I JUST GRADUATED . . .
NOW WHAT?

I JUST GRADUATED... NOW WHAT?

Honest Answers from Those
Who Have Been There

KATHERINE SCHWARZENEGGER

CROWN ARCHETYPE
New York

Published in the United States by Crown Archetype, an imprint
of the Crown Publishing Group, a division of Random House
LLC, a Penguin Random House Company, New York.
www.crownpublishing.com

Crown Archetype and colophon is a registered trademark of
Random House LLC.

Library of Congress Cataloging-in-Publication data is available
upon request.

ISBN 978-0-385-34720-4
eBook ISBN 978-0-385-34721-1

Printed in the United States of America

Jacket design by Jessie Sayward Bright

10 9 8 7 6 5 4 3 2 1

First Edition

I dedicate this book to every person being asked the world's most annoying question;

"SO NOW WHAT ARE YOU GOING TO DO?"

Whether you're facing that dreaded question after high school, college, or quitting a job, have faith that you will figure it out and that you are not the first person to be in the position that you are in right now. There have been many people before you, and will be many after, who feel like they have no idea what to do with their life. Just breathe (and read this book). You will know what to do when the time is right. Good luck!

Contents

INTRODUCTION   I

Anderson Cooper   25
*"THE PEOPLE I ADMIRE MOST HADN'T
REALLY FOLLOWED A PARTICULAR PATH."*

Eva Longoria   35
"YOUR DEGREE IS JUST A STEPPING-STONE."

John Legend   45
"IT'S NOT WRONG TO BE AFRAID."

Sara Blakely   51
*"IF I HADN'T BOMBED OUT ON THE LSAT EXAM, I
WOULD NEVER HAVE REDIRECTED
MY LIFE TO COME UP WITH SPANX."*

Blake Mycoskie   63
*"WHEN YOU ARE GOOD AT SOMETHING,
THE MONEY ALWAYS FOLLOWS."*

Jennifer Meyer   69
*"WHAT'S BETTER THAN BLOWING MONEY
ON YOUR DREAM?"*

Bear Grylls   75
*"THE PATH LESS TRAVELED ALWAYS MAKES
FOR A MORE INTERESTING JOURNEY."*

CONTENTS

Lauren Bush Lauren   79
"IT MAY TAKE THREE OR FOUR JOBS TO DISCOVER YOUR TRUE CAREER PATH."

Brad Wollack   85
"IT'S IMPORTANT TO FIND ONE PERSON WHO BELIEVES IN YOU."

Jillian Michaels   93
"REJECTION IS GOD'S PROTECTION."

Andy Cohen   101
"WHEN I GOT MY FIRST JOB, I FELT LIKE A SUCCESS FOR GETTING THAT JOB, AND EVERY JOB I'VE HAD SINCE. . . ."

Nicole Williams   109
"GET PAST THE EXCUSES, NEWS, UNEMPLOYMENT RATE, AND STATISTICS."

Armin van Buuren   119
"YOU NEED DISCIPLINE IF YOU WANT SOMETHING IN LIFE, AND THEN YOU NEED A PLAN TO GET IT."

Meghan McCain   127
"I CONSIDER MYSELF MILDLY SUCCESSFUL BECAUSE I HAVE BEEN ABLE TO CONTINUE DOING THE THINGS I LOVE. . . ."

Jared Eng   133
"YOU ARE IN THE WRONG ROOM IF YOU ARE THE SMARTEST PERSON IN THE ROOM."

Laysha Ward   139
"LEAVE THINGS BETTER THAN YOU FOUND THEM."

Darren Hardy   149
"GO AFTER IT AND NEVER LOOK BACK."

CONTENTS

Alli Webb   161

"PURSUE WHAT YOU WANT AND NOT WHAT YOUR PARENTS WANT YOU TO DO."

Adam Braun   173

"THERE IS A TIME AND PLACE TO CHOOSE MONEY OVER A LEARNING ENVIRONMENT, BUT YOU DO THAT WHEN THE MARGIN IS VERY BIG, AND THAT DOESN'T HAPPEN RIGHT OUT OF SCHOOL."

Maria Shriver   181

"WORK HARD, BE LUCKY, BE AWAKE, AND NEVER THINK YOU ARE TOO GOOD TO DO X, Y, AND Z."

Matt Barkley   193

"THE REAL WORLD CAN BE HARD AT TIMES, BUT I DON'T THINK PEOPLE ARE WILLING TO SACRIFICE ENOUGH. . . ."

Cristina Carlino   197

"IF YOU CAN'T HANDLE FAILURE OR BEING WRONG, YOU WILL NEVER SUCCEED."

Mike Swift   203

"START A MOVEMENT, NOT A TREND."

Serena Williams   211

"IT'S IMPORTANT TO PAY ATTENTION TO THINGS THAT MAKE YOU HAPPY. YOUR QUALITY OF LIFE DEPENDS ON YOUR ATTITUDE TOWARD THE THINGS THAT HAPPEN TO YOU."

Arnold Schwarzenegger   215

"THE MOST IMPORTANT THING FOR ALL OF US IS NOT MONEY. IT IS FEELING PRODUCTIVE."

Gayle King   223

"YOU WON'T LOVE EVERY JOB YOU HAVE OVER THE YEARS, AND YOU'RE NOT SUPPOSED TO."

Candace Nelson   231
*"YOU DON'T BECOME AN ENTREPRENEUR IF YOU
DON'T APPRECIATE A CHALLENGE."*

Ron Bergum   239
*"ONCE YOU GRADUATE, FINANCIAL
INDEPENDENCE IS YOUR OBLIGATION."*

Ben Kaufman   247
*"UNDERSTANDING WHY THINGS SUCCEED
AND FAIL IS THE BEST SORT OF LEARNING
YOU CAN DO."*

Joe Kakaty
Dealing with College Loan Debt   255
*"BE REALISTIC: VACATION OR SPRING BREAK, A
CELL PHONE, AND CABLE TV ARE LUXURIES, NOT
NECESSITIES."*

Dr. Dan Siegel   259
*When Moving Home Meets
Mixed Emotions*

LEARNING THE ROPES   269

NOW WHAT?   271

ACKNOWLEDGMENTS   277

Introduction

"Oh shit! I just graduated . . . *Now* what?"

That was the overwhelming thought running through my head on the day I walked across the stage and received my diploma in communications from the Annenberg School at the University of Southern California. As I said good-bye to my friends and teachers, I felt terrified about closing the chapter and opening a new chapter in the real world. There were no feelings of great elation or relief among the many hugs and cheers. Instead, there was a feeling of total panic and paralyzing fear of the unknown. Picture a frozen smile on the outside melting into panic on the inside. Of course I was happy to be done with school, but I was in an unexpected state of shock. Every hug and congratulations on my graduation was complete with the question "What's next?" The ink wasn't even dry on my diploma!

I know life is riddled with tough questions whose answers we don't always know off the top of our heads. And the reality is, we will face these kinds of questions for most of our lives. It started when I was a junior in high school. It seemed everywhere I went, people asked me, "What did you get on the SAT?" "How did you do?" "Have you applied to college?" "What college are you planning to attend?" "Where are you going?" "What schools did you get accepted to?"

Before being accepted to any colleges, I remember feeling lost and unsure because I didn't know where I would end up after high school graduation. Rejection letters came, and so did acceptance letters. The University of Southern California was always at the top of my list, so as long as I was accepted, that would be my school of choice. After a lot of anxiety, USC accepted me. When I made my decision, I thought I'd gotten a reprieve from the annoying "What's next?" questions, only to have them start again my junior year of college. "What will you do when you graduate?" "Did you get a job yet?" "Where are you going to live?"

The closer graduation got, "What are you going to do now?" seemed to follow me wherever I went. I had been in school for so long, always going, studying, working, and volunteering. I was that annoying perfectionist who challenged myself to write a book, while in college, about women's body image, something I and every girl struggles with. To say I spread myself thin doesn't begin to describe how I felt during that time. In fact, at the beginning of my senior year, I felt like I was on autopilot. I planned to move to New York, get a job working in television, and continue my go-go-go mentality.

But as my graduation neared, I began to hear a little voice inside me telling me, "Slow down, stop, whoa, take a beat, what are you doing?"

I was like, *Huh? Who is that?*

What the . . . ?

I had never done that.

I am the kind of person who thrives on staying busy. I had my first job working in a boutique when I was fifteen and have always enjoyed working. I'd always had a clear vision of what my future looked like. From my earliest memories in elementary school, I plotted my course through middle school, high school, college, and beyond— right into my thirties. (Trust me, I am not the only person who does this. Most girls have their wedding planned in high school, right down to their dream husband, dream house, dream baby, and dream career that allows for all of this to happen! Guys I've spoken with have their own version of this too!) I could envision every aspect of my life that whole time, but I never planned on this confusing doubt, uncertainty, angst, and fear after college where for the first time in my life, there was absolutely nothing to see.

As graduation approached, this tight-knot feeling about my future grew. Tums became my best friend. Luckily, my other best friend is my mom. We are very close and can talk about everything in an open and honest way. I told her how I was feeling confused and lost because I wasn't sure about my next steps. I shared my fear about the unknown. Throughout my entire life, everything had always been planned out and there was always an order for what would come next. But now for the first time, there wasn't any concrete plan for what I was "supposed to do" next, and that terrified me. So when I told my mom that I wasn't sure what I wanted to do after graduating, instead of putting pressure on me, she eased my stress by telling me it was okay to take a beat. She suggested that I might just pause for the summer and revisit the "now what" question after Labor Day.

"*Pause. Now there's an idea,*" I thought.

The idea of "pausing" wasn't something I could really wrap my head around. I honestly didn't even know if I could actually do that. I knew that "pausing" wasn't something I felt I was programmed to do, but I wanted to explore it. Every time I told my mom I was worried, she assured me that she felt the same way when she graduated and that this fear happens to a lot of people—in fact, it happened to her. When my mom graduated from Georgetown University, she told me that she was also scared. She said that every time someone asked her, "Now what?" she beat herself up over not having THE answer. My mom even told me that she would make up stuff and began telling people she was going to law school even though she had no plans to go, just so they would be quiet. She made up this excuse just to keep people from asking her the question. Knowing she went through the same thing helped me in my search for my answer to the question.

In fact, my mom took this concept of pausing and made it her theme when she gave the commencement speech at my graduation from the Annenberg School at

USC in May 2012, in which she offered the following advice to all of us listening that day:

> . . . I know right now everybody's asking you those same questions: "What are you going to do after graduation? Do you have a job? Where will you be working? How much are they paying? Where are you going? Where will you be living? Who are you seeing?" Oh, my God—so many questions!
>
> And here you are: sitting there ready to hit the Fast Forward button and find out the answers. I get that. I was just LIKE you: I lived on Fast Forward.
>
> But today, I have one wish for you. Before you go out and press that Fast Forward button, I'm hoping—I'm praying—that you'll have the courage to first press the Pause button.
>
> That's right: the Pause button. I hope if you learn anything from me today, you learn and remember . . . The Power of the Pause.
>
> Pausing allows you to take a beat—to take a breath in your life. As everybody else is rushing around like a lunatic out there, I dare you to do the opposite.

I, like my friends who were all sitting in the room intently taking in her message that memorable day, realized that what my mom was encouraging us to do was the absolute perfect advice. She spoke about how the question "What are you going to do?" follows us our whole lives. It comes in many forms, but it's always there. No matter what you do, or how much you accomplish, there will always be someone there to ask you, "So what now?"

"When are you going to get a promotion?"

"When are you getting married?"

"When are you going to have a baby?"

"When are you going to have another baby?"

And so on . . .

The reality of having to face the "What's next?" question for the rest of my life was overwhelming. At the time, I could barely figure out my plans for the weekend, let alone the next phase of my life, so after graduation, whenever someone asked me about my plans, I simply responded with, "I'm pausing."

It worked like a charm every time! No one questioned it. If anything, I think people were so shocked by my response that they didn't know how to follow up with anything else but, "Oh, good for you." Most people nodded in confusion or just told me how cool it was to realize that right now is such an important time to sit back and reflect. I actually got kind of a kick out of watching people's reactions when I told them about my pausing plan; it was clearly not what they were expecting to hear from me.

The pausing response quickly caught on with most of my friends too. They all began calling me to say they were using the "I'm pausing" line, while their parents were calling my mother to ask, "Are you crazy, telling these kids to stop and take a beat?" Some people couldn't understand the value in taking a moment to figure things out. My mom explained what she meant in her speech:

. . . It's really important to pause along the way and take a break from communicating outwardly, so you can communicate inwardly, with yourself.

PAUSE—and take the time to find out what's important to you. Find out what you love, what's real and true to you—so it can infuse and inform your work and make it your own. . . .

And if you don't have a job yet and someone asks you, "What are you going to do?" Just pause, and be aware of this fundamental truth: It's okay not to know what you're going to do! It's okay not to have all the answers. You don't have to be like I was at your age and beat yourself up for not knowing.

It's okay to go with the truth and tell people, "You know what? It's a tough job market out there. I'm not sure what I'm going to be doing. I'm pausing, I'm open, and I'm looking at my options."

. . . I didn't invent this stop-everything and pause idea.

Jesus fasted for forty days and nights in the desert. Henry David Thoreau went to Walden Pond. Anne Morrow Lindbergh went to sea. Buddha, Gandhi, Mother Teresa—the greatest and wisest have often stopped and withdrawn from active lives to journey within themselves. The wisdom they garnered there and shared with us has impacted the world.

Now, I know I am lucky to come from a family who could support me in my summer of "pauses" while I found my way. I decided to move out of the apartment I was sharing with my best friend before graduation and move back home. My parents had recently separated and I wanted to move back home with my mom and my siblings. I hadn't planned on moving home after college, but a big part of me loved being around my family, so the idea of moving back home with them didn't sound so bad. Still, although my intentions were good, it felt like a step backward for me. You spend your whole life taking the proper steps into adulthood, and there I was, a college graduate, living at home with my family. Most of my friends had their own apartments and were living their own lives, and I was struggling and conflicted with my decision—big-time.

My parents weren't forcing me to go out and get a job right away, but they made sure I also knew that they weren't the type to support me sitting around doing nothing as my job. They understood and supported my need to stop, think, and discover what it is I am looking for. Besides, I definitely inherited their strong work ethic, so I don't think they thought I was being a slacker. They could see I was just confused. As it turns out, I wasn't alone. Almost all of my peers were feeling the same way.

This universal feeling got me thinking, "There should be a book out there with advice and tips from people who have been there, who can relate to how so many of us feel because they have been in the same position, and can help recent graduates answer the 'Now what?' question." After all, it's a different environment for those of us who are graduating. The job market and the economy make things really challenging. So many kids are graduating with huge student loans looming over their heads and great uncertainty about how they will pay them back without a job.

Many of us feel like it's difficult for our parents to understand our generation. They don't understand the different career opportunities we have today or that we don't want to go to work at one place for many years and end up unhappy with our career choices. In fact, a recent survey of working people showed that a whopping 70 percent weren't happy in their jobs, with the main reasons being cited as a difficult boss and no room for growth. Today, my generation is lucky enough to choose what kind of job environment we want to work in and the kind of life we want to live, all because our parents' generation worked so hard to give that to us.

There's a perception that the moment you graduate from college, you are officially ready to enter the real world. I think that concept is unfair and unrealistic. Sure, there's a lot of posturing that you are self-assured and secure with your plans when in fact, most people aren't. A lot of people talk about the jobs they have lined up, the great opportunities that exist out there, and how they plan to seek them out. And for some, that may be true. For the majority of us, though, it's the furthest thing from the truth. We all decided to go to college as the next step after high school in order to prepare ourselves for life in the real world. We spent four years of our lives going to classes and being prepped for real-life situations so by the time graduation came around, we would feel ready to deal with life head-on. But not so fast!

Whenever I heard my friends talking about the jobs they had planned after college, it made me feel worse about myself because they seemingly had their lives together and I felt I didn't. Since I had no plan in place after graduating, I was forced to give up my comfortable view of myself as someone who had it together. This was a really painful and challenging realization. Sacrificing who I thought I was became a big deal because I usually have a strong sense of who I am, and the idea that I would have to change that didn't sit well with me. For the first time in my life, I was the planner . . . *with no plan*. Worse, I had no idea where to start. All of a sudden, there wasn't anything I felt a calling for, and though I was very proud to have accomplished so much leading up to graduation, I felt like I needed a time-out to really consider my options.

The one question that kept creeping into my mind was "How can you make a plan when you don't know what you are planning for?" The funny thing about being able to see things in your future is that first you need to be able to have a vision for what direction you want to go.

I was stuck, and I couldn't budge.

So June came and went.

Then July and August passed too.

I got more stuck.

I had given myself a "pause" expiration date of early September—right around the time most kids are going back to school and people get back into the grind of things. I wasn't exactly sitting around doing nothing, but I had a constant nagging feeling, which never seemed to dissipate, that I should be doing more. I appeared busy: going to meetings, doing research on possible jobs that would interest me. I spent most of that time asking myself some tough questions about what really makes me happy.

While promoting my first book, I realized how much I loved doing television work and wanted to continue to explore the TV world while I was in college. I had done some freelance work on television, for *Extra* and *Entertainment Tonight* and knew that I loved doing that, but for whatever reason, I wouldn't allow myself to turn that into my career yet. It was almost like I couldn't clearly envision that for my future. I was interested in political and lifestyle stories. I love the talk show format and even had the chance to co-host *Anderson Live,* the syndicated daytime talk show, in the fall of 2012. That was the closest I came to finding my passion during these months. I knew that the general direction I wanted to go was to someday be in front of the camera, perhaps doing a talk show, or create some type of lifestyle brand that inspires others in my generation to be their very best. I began questioning whether staying in Los Angeles was the right direction or whether a little time in New York might help give me some distance from my familiar, comfortable environment. I had stayed in New York for three months when I did an internship for Dove after my freshman year of college and when I worked for CNN the following summer. I had a pretty good idea of what being away from home felt like, but the commitment to make the permanent move paralyzed me with fear. To be fair, moving to New York without a job wasn't an ideal situation to be in either, so that held me back too.

Even though I lived away from home during my college years, USC was in close proximity to my parents. On any given day, I could be in our family kitchen within an hour. I will admit, I went home often throughout my college years. I am one of those kids who actually enjoy spending quality time with their family and thrive on being around them. It's one of the reasons I decided to go to school so close to home.

Although I was active, I was still pretty hard on myself, believing that others were judging me for not having it all figured out. Even if they weren't saying it, I felt as if people were thinking, "What is she doing and why isn't she doing more?" That voice in my head made me feel embarrassed and got me down. In retrospect, I can't say that anyone was really thinking that about me—except, perhaps, me.

By the time November rolled around, I was in full-on depression mode. Not having school to fall back on felt totally unnatural and really uncomfortable. I'd lost all of the dreams about my future, which felt like it had been put on temporary hold. I'd gotten to such a low place in my life that I didn't want to work out (something I used to be passionate about), and I'd stopped dreaming of having my own place because I was still living at home. I wasn't dating, was being completely antisocial, and felt as though I had nothing substantial happening in my life that made me feel good, and no project I could sink my teeth into and call my own. It was the first time in my life I had no energy; I actually felt lazy and had zero motivation. This was definitely the darkest time of my life. I felt super sad about everything—especially my future.

In an effort to help me get out of my funk, my mom took me to meditation classes and even to a horse whisperer. She finally decided that both of us should go to a Tony Robbins seminar called "Date with Destiny" that was taking place in Palm Springs in late November. Date with Destiny is about understanding why you feel and behave the way you do. The six-day seminar promised to teach us ways to live a happier life filled with love, passion, and success moving forward.

When my mom first suggested this, I said absolutely not. I told her I wasn't experiencing a midlife crisis, and I had labeled those seminars as being for people who were in much more confusing periods of their lives but were motivated to learn. After some convincing from my mom, I told her I would go. Although I initially agreed to go to "support" my mom, I can now admit that these tools were exactly what I needed to kick-start the next phase of my life.

Although I was able to attend only two days of the six-day Tony Robbins seminar, it was a life-altering experience. Most people there were a lot older than me and going through very challenging times in their lives. Tony spoke a lot about the stories we tell ourselves, the things we say, think, or feel, whether they're true or not. He also talked about how most people make up excuses to avoid facing the truth. That message really resonated with me. I've never been an excuse maker and have always been frustrated by people who are. In a way, I had become that kind of person, and that realization wasn't good, but it was definitely freeing.

Tony doesn't sugarcoat anything—he just says it like it is. I have a great appreciation for that trait in people, even if what they have to say is often very hard to hear. When Tony spoke to different people one-on-one in front of the hundreds of attendees in the room, I learned something valuable from each person's experiences and how Tony broke it down to find a reasonable and logical resolution.

During my time there, I had to look at my life in a way that I had never done before. I had to go deep in my head and heart to figure out what I wanted to do with my life and what I was going to do differently to get there. By the time my mom and I left the seminar, I felt like a huge weight had been lifted off my shoulders and that I was seeing things from a whole new perspective. I was a different person. I felt clear in my head and confident that even though I didn't have a step-by-step plan for myself right away, I was getting close and I needed to trust that I would get there.

When I had the chance to meet with Tony afterward one-on-one, he called me out on my frustration and what he referred to as me carrying around a "masculine mask." Ouch. He said this façade was the reason I felt annoyed all of the time, which was creating toxicity in my life, instead of letting my softer, more feminine side shine through. What I realized was that being pissed off and frustrated about things happening around me wasn't making things any better. It made me feel powerless. It certainly wasn't having a positive impact on the relationships in my life that were making me angry. If anything, my attitude was making those relationships worse. Tony explained that I had to take off this mask and change my energy from negative into positive so I could draw the things I really wanted toward me instead of pushing them away. It was definitely time to leave my negative emotional baggage behind, and I decided then that I would not be bringing it back to Los Angeles with me! When I returned to L.A., somehow I felt happier and lighter, like I had left all my worries and struggles behind, and I was ready for a fresh start.

I am a huge believer that everything happens for a reason. After my Date with Destiny experience, I was certain that I would start working in early January. I vowed to stop being sad and feeling sorry for myself because it's not really who I am. When I got home, I decided to make my first vision board to help me create a picture for my dreams so I could actually see all of the things I really wanted in life. I included a house, a wedding photo, a picture with a family in it, a picture of the ocean, and a picture of a group of people having a fun dinner, along with pictures of Oprah Winfrey, Ellen DeGeneres, and Tyra Banks because I want to be the next generation's talk show host, just as each of them were for their generation. I cut out a TV and wrote the word *Youth* on it so I would always be able to relate to my generation and focus on our needs.

It finally dawned on me that if I was feeling this uncomfortable moving forward after college, lots of other people were most likely equally confused, stuck, disoriented, and terrified too. We find ourselves confused when we don't know how to go about navigating the real world after college. We think that by spending four years of our lives in school we will be properly prepared, but we're not at all. I decided that the best way to slay my fear and help others at the same time was to face it head-on.

I came up with the idea to interview other people about their experiences out there in the real world and ask them for their best advice on managing the unknown. I thought, "If I can pick the brains of some of the most brilliant thinkers and business leaders about how they found the courage to walk their path, face adversity head-on, and overcome rejection, fear, and bad choices, then I can make a giant leap into my own future without making the same mistakes along the way." The funny thing about struggling is that when you tell people how alone you feel with your struggles, you end up finding out that they once felt the same way and yet managed to find a way out. I figured if so many people were feeling this way now and so many successful people had felt that way in the past, why not shed light on the issue and talk about it?

I wanted to know what they would tell our generation, and I was curious about the lessons they learned along the way that helped make them successful. I thought I could compile all of this information into a book and share my findings with others who are feeling the same way I did.

———————

Not getting a job right out of college felt like the lowest point in my life, but what it really did was force me to learn so much about myself. In retrospect, I wouldn't have changed a moment, because those low experiences brought me to the here and now and to writing this book.

For most of us, life after graduation may be the first time we have to financially support ourselves, budget our finances, take on real responsibilities, and create a life outside the safety of the cocoon we felt protected by during our school years. Perhaps like I did, you think everyone else has got it all together while you don't.

What I've learned from the interviews is that all experiences are good experiences, even the ones that don't feel good in the moment. Sometimes the wrong job can open the right door; every situation has potential. The only thing you have to lose by not getting out there is opportunity.

Millennials have been plagued by stereotypes such as being too tech-obsessed, entitled, and lazy. Many people think we don't have a strong work ethic or the persistence necessary to succeed. This perception of the millennial generation is so rampant that companies such as Merrill Lynch and Ernst & Young have hired consultants to teach them how to deal with us. Ask anyone in middle management today what their biggest issue is in finding solid young employees, and they will immediately say, "Their sense of entitlement!" It appears that our generation comes off as if we really don't want to work that hard.

I disagree.

I am not afraid of working hard, and for the most part, neither are my friends and our peer groups. The definition of hard work hasn't really changed so much as the venue in which we can accomplish things in less time because of technology and ease of access to information—something our parents' generation didn't have. While I started out believing that my generation's work ethic was really no different from the ones before us, I've come to realize that in many ways it is. I believe the millennial generation brings a lot to the table. Despite the notion that we don't want to work or have unrealistic expectations, there are those in the workplace who see our resourcefulness as an asset and who understand that the tools we bring to the table will not only help bring their businesses into the next millennium, but are critical to their success because we know how to get things done in a new and more efficient way.

According to a UNC Kenan-Flagler Business School and YEC study, millennials are highly ambitious, with most placing a tremendous emphasis on finding jobs with their best chances for career and personal growth. Hiring an employee who is active in social media greatly increases a company's digital reach. Millennials switch their attention between media platforms such as laptops, smartphones, tablets, and television on average 27 times an hour. Not only do millennials multitask far more than previous generations, they value social media freedom, device flexibility, and work mobility over salary when accepting a job offer.

Most of us don't see the path toward our future as an easy one because the current statistics tell us it's not. Those of us looking to enter the job market will face a harder time finding jobs, let alone the career we were looking for, but it doesn't mean you can't work toward your dream. In fact, for many, statistics show that you won't zero in on the job that is right for you until at least age twenty-six or twenty-seven—the age at which many sociologists believe people transition from young adult into adulthood.

In 2014, millennials will make up 36 percent of the workforce, with that number increasing to 46 percent by 2020. Companies that are growing will come to depend on this generation, the most diverse ever to enter the marketplace and who place their highest value on joining a company where they have the opportunity for personal development, career growth, and then financial stability. This means that whatever you choose to do in the future, you are an important asset to the right company.

Writing this book began as a resource to help me figure out my next steps. It morphed into the most incredible learning experience I could have ever wished for while navigating my own path toward a fulfilling and meaningful career.

Some of the people I interviewed were just entering the workforce, while others have been in it for many years.

Some have only an undergraduate degree, while some have a master's degree in business or other areas. Others never went to college, or did go but for whatever reason did not graduate. The advent of social media and other technology as a primary platform for business is why I also wanted to talk to young entrepreneurs who are the real difference makers in today's society. They each started with an idea and were willing to pursue it despite people telling them it couldn't be done. Each of their real-world experiences and insights illuminated the process of what it takes to make it out there, in the job market and in life. Most important, almost everyone I spoke to shared their experience of feeling lost and confused after college or at some point in their life. Hearing their stories made me feel so much better about my journey.

The most common advice that came from almost everyone I spoke to was to find a job you're passionate about doing, which is usually easier said than done. If you can create a career built on passion, your chances for success, fulfillment, and longevity are far greater than if you take any old job simply for the paycheck. Amazingly, everyone had something different to offer—which helped broaden my perspective on what's really important when weighing my various options. Though there have been many takeaways from interviewing everyone in this book, for me, one of the biggest has been embracing the opportunities we have. Hard work and struggling are an important part of the journey, but we can get there. There are so many different types of jobs that simply didn't exist in previous generations. For example, my mom didn't have the ability to say she wanted to start a "lifestyle brand" when she graduated. For her to achieve that goal, she would have needed to work for a major corporation and carve out a niche for herself instead of creating it through social media and other creative outlets available today.

Writing this book also helped me narrow down what I want to do and then understand the steps I would need to take to get me there. Since I began writing this book in January 2013, I've taken a leap of faith into my future by creating my own lifestyle website, a place where I blog about current issues, interests, and ideas that feel relevant for my generation as well as exploring my career in television. I have never been busier and couldn't be happier with the outcome of my efforts or the journey that led me here. I finally have purpose, passion, and great pleasure in the work I am doing back in my life.

We all need to get to a place of being comfortable with ourselves and how we are choosing to live our lives. I haven't met a single person who doesn't still feel overwhelmed by the "Now what?" questions we will experience for the rest of our lives; sadly it is endless. I do hope that by reading this book, people will become more aware of the nagging question and learn to handle it without feeling that they should be doing something more. Knowing that so many people have had their own unique way of finding their path in life is encouraging.

I am so pleased to share all of the information and lessons I've learned through the interviews that follow in this book. Each story of their failures and successes, their perseverance and fortitude, and their strength and courage inspired me to get out of my rut and into the game. It took some time to discover my path, but in the end, it was truly worth it. And I am just beginning. I am aware that I will never stop "figuring myself out" and trying to understand the future.

So if you're feeling confused and uncertain about your future and career, it's okay. Pause. Take a beat. Look at it as finishing one chapter in your life and starting another. As you read each person's amazing journey in this book, I hope you will pause. Each person who contributed to this book agreed to participate because they wished they'd had a book like this when they were starting out. Based on their stories and experiences they each share, take comfort in knowing that it's okay if you're feeling like everyone else has their life together and you don't, because the reality is that they probably feel the same way. Everyone finds their way on their own time. Life is a marathon, not a sprint. Pace yourself for the road that lies ahead and don't worry if you don't have all of the answers right away. They will come, so be patient and enjoy the process.

INTERVIEWS

Anderson Cooper

"The people I admire most hadn't really followed a particular path that was visible when they were on it."

COLLEGE ATTENDED: Yale University, bachelor's degree in liberal arts

OCCUPATION: Broadcast journalist, author, talk show host

I first met Anderson Cooper when I was asked to co-host his syndicated daytime talk show in the fall of 2012. Although we have mutual friends, we had never met before that day, but I always loved Anderson on TV and think he is great at what he does, so I was excited to do the show. When you co-host his show, the producers don't have you socialize with Anderson beforehand because they want a natural flow of banter when you go on the air. About fifteen minutes before we were set to go live, I was directed into his office to say hello. I was nervous and thrilled about being on the show and about the possible topics we might cover in our conversation. Anderson spoke to me in such a kind and genuinely caring manner. He assured me that he wanted my time to be a great experience—one I could look back on with appreciation instead of regret. It was such a relief to hear him talk to me on a human level and to know he was interested in what I was doing with my life. His manner calmed me, and after we talked, it was as if all of my nervousness disappeared and all I could feel was excitement.

Anderson's story is one of great strength, courage, and character. Like me, he felt lost, insecure, and indecisive after college. He was terrified about being thrown into the real world with no set plan. It gave him anxiety and he felt intimidated by the people around him planning their career. After college, Anderson fell into several random jobs, including doing carpentry work and waiting tables.

Anderson was brutally honest with me. He confessed that the sudden and tragic death of his twenty-three-year-old brother, who was just two years older than Anderson, inspired him to look deep within himself to figure out what he really wanted out of life. In order to give himself time to heal and reflect, Anderson traveled to Southeast Asia and thought about what interested him the most. He made a list of what he wanted in a career and what he didn't want, which I think is a great thing to do. When he studied the lists, he realized he possessed a passion for survival and understanding why some people survive and others don't, which led him to wanting to work as a correspondent. He couldn't get a job right away with a major network, so he became a fact checker at an independent news network for youth called Channel One. After some time there, he realized that job wasn't sending him in the right direction for what he wanted to do in the future. He wanted to travel, go into war zones to report on people fighting for what they believed in and on horrific situations happening around the world. It was a struggle for Anderson to get hired as a correspondent, so he created a position to do it on his own, which is what a lot of people graduating college deal with today. In Anderson's mind, there wasn't anything to lose when it came to his career, so he decided to be proactive and make the most of his situation, which ended up working out pretty well.

One of the reasons Anderson agreed to do an interview with me for this book was that he had wanted to write something similar when he graduated from college. He completely related to the struggle we face about what to do next and thought he could help others figure it out by talking about the issue. Even though he didn't end up writing his book, he has some amazing life lessons to offer to people through his experiences right out of school, many of which you will read in his story.

I had a bunch of odd jobs in college, but none of them brought me any closer to knowing what I wanted to do when I graduated. I didn't apply for any jobs during my senior year because I was confused about my future. My brother committed suicide about a month before I started my senior year, which was kind of a blur for me because I didn't understand why he did it.

I wanted to figure out what to do with my life, so I took a year off after graduation and continued to work a few jobs here and there. I liked doing carpentry work and did a couple of jobs out on Long Island for a while. I also traveled around Southeast Asia with some friends. Taking that time was important to me for many reasons. It helped me because I was going through a rough period, trying to get a perspective on what kind of person I wanted to be and the life I wanted to lead. I was also trying to understand what happened to my brother. There I was, interested in survival, and my brother committed suicide. The whole notion of why some people survive and some people don't was an overwhelming question floating through my head.

The year off I took after college was the most terrifying and intimidating period in my life. I think it is for a lot of people. For two or three years after graduating college, I felt like any choice I made wasn't taking me down a road I wanted to be on. It was cutting off options instead of creating opportunities. I had this notion that I had to be on some sort of definitive path, some call it a "career path," and if I took a step down any road, it didn't necessarily lead me somewhere. Instead, it sealed off other roads that I could have gone down. Looking back, I now know that isn't the case, but it took some time and talking to some adults who had achieved some level of success for me to realize there is no clear-cut path—especially today. To create clarity, the only thing I could do at the time was make a list of all of the things I wanted out of life. When I had that complete, I compared it to the list I'd made of possible jobs I wanted. Travel was important to me. I didn't want to be stuck in a cubicle when I was sixty-five years old, wearing a gray suit. My lists showed me a lot of things I didn't want to do, which left me with no other alternative than figuring out what I really wanted. When I analyzed both lists, being a reporter fit the things I wanted most—especially being a foreign correspondent.

I watched a lot of TV news growing up and had always been interested in it. I attempted to get an entry-level job at ABC in their news division, but they had a hiring freeze on because there was a recession at the time. I applied to CBS too, but couldn't get hired there either. I became hugely discouraged. I thought not being hired by one of the networks was cataclysmic, and I was desperate. In hindsight, it was the best thing that ever happened because had I gotten the entry-level jobs at ABC or CBS, I would never have become a correspondent. The movement inside a network news organization is glacial. It takes forever to get promoted out of those jobs. There certainly isn't much of a path from being a desk assistant to becoming a correspondent.

After several months of searching, I finally got a job as a fact checker at a company called Channel One, which was a twelve-minute news program with two minutes of commercials that was made for schools. Channel One aired in about half of the high schools and middle schools in America. I spent six months working as a fact checker before realizing that being cooped up in an office wasn't for me. I wanted to be a reporter, out traveling and seeing the world. I wouldn't get there by being a fact checker, and I was pretty sure my bosses would never see me as anything but a fact checker. If I wanted them to see me in a different way, I was going to have to change their perception. If I put myself into an exciting or dangerous situation where there was a story, I would be able to shoot and tell that story.

I was in a lucky position. I didn't have student loans to pay back, so that pressure was off, but I had made a deal with my mom that once I graduated from college, I was on my own. I had been working as a model from the time I was ten or eleven years old, which was confusing and embarrassing, but it paid well, so I had money saved up. I have always been obsessed with earning my own money and being independent. I was willing to tap into my savings to do something I believed in. I came up with the idea to quit my job at Channel One and just start traveling to war zones to cover stories on my own. I'd travel light—just me, a camera, and a fake press pass a friend of mine put together. I told my boss what my plan was and said I'd give him the first look at my footage and stories. If he liked it, he could put it on the air. I figured it would be harder for him to say no because the company was not liable for my safety or paying for my insurance. If I got killed, it wasn't on them because they didn't send me there. I became a self-appointed correspondent going to places I wanted to report on. All I needed was a camera I could take with me, which my boss agreed I could take from them.

The first destination on my journey was Burma. I'd read a story about some students there who were fighting the Burmese government. I had no previous experience in front of a camera before this, but I could write copy and knew how to shoot video. I didn't think telling the story would be hard. I was by myself, so I had to turn on the camera, face it toward me, and talk. Sometimes I'd even ask someone else to hold it while I did my piece. I was sleeping outside and on rooftops. I didn't have any money and wasn't eating very much. It was a dangerous situation, but it was something I was passionate about and I was willing to accept the risk because I found the story meaningful and compelling.

I got the story in Burma and sent it back to New York. Unfortunately, the piece wasn't enough to get me hired, but I headed to Vietnam for a while and shot an additional four or five stories. Channel One still didn't hire me. Six months later, I told my boss that I was going to Africa and would guarantee *ten* stories over the course of three months. For whatever reason, my boss agreed to that idea and let me run with it. The first big story I shot was on the famine in Somalia, in 1992. By this time, I had developed a natural ease in front of the camera and an organic style of shooting footage—which is pretty much what I still do today. I felt like I had nothing to lose and no other options and simply did what felt right. My story had a big impact on the Channel One audience. The response was so positive that my boss formally hired me full time to be their foreign correspondent for the next three years.

Even though I didn't get hired at ABC for an entry-level job, three years after being at Channel One, they hired me as a correspondent for the network. That is pretty much unheard of, because at twenty-seven I was the youngest guy hired at ABC since Peter Jennings, who was hired at twenty-six, and Ted Koppel, who was twenty-three when he was hired for ABC Radio News.

When I look back on those couple of years after college, it sucked. I hated my feelings of insecurity and indecision. My mom told me to "Follow my bliss." It's a line from Joseph Campbell when he was being interviewed by Bill Moyers that a lot of people use. It is a hard thing to do if you've got heavy student loans to pay or aren't sure what your bliss is. If, however, you are able to follow your bliss, I believe this is where true success—however you define success—comes from because it allows you to work harder than anyone else around you. Doing what you love doesn't feel like work—it feels like an extension of yourself. It's the way I feel about what I do now.

There is a line from Lawrence of Arabia, one of my favorite films: "Nothing is written." Lawrence says this because he is constantly being told that "it is written" and "this will happen this way." Rest assured, you write your own story. Knowing that gives me hope because it makes me feel that with luck and determination you can write your own ticket—or story. The things that seemed so important when I was in college and the year or two that followed, from the classes I was taking to what my major was, I can barely remember now. Throughout my career,

I have never had anyone in a job interview ask to see my college transcript. All of that seemed important at the time, and I suppose it was—but not *that* important in the grand scheme of things.

I am always a little wary telling people what to do with their lives because circumstances are different for everyone. I know a lot of people who weren't sure what to do after graduating who ran off to graduate school or law school to avoid figuring it all out. Today, many of them are very unhappy lawyers.

Eva Longoria

"Look for a job, invest in your career."

COLLEGE ATTENDED: Texas A&M University, bachelor's degree in kinesiology; California State University, Northridge, master's degree in Chicano studies

OCCUPATION: Actress, political advocate

When you think of Eva Longoria, you think of her beauty, talent, and passion. But she is also someone who constantly wants to broaden her knowledge and awareness of what's going on in the world. I find myself very inspired by Eva's philanthropic generosity and her interest in advocating for the Chicano community. When I spoke with Eva, she shared with me that she had a sister with intellectual disabilities who has taught her so much about life. She spoke about how much her sister means to her family and the lessons she has learned from watching her over the years. Eva and her entire family are involved with "Special Olympics," an organization my grandmother started and that I'm involved in too.

I never realized how hard Eva has worked to achieve all she has accomplished in her acting, political interests, and charity work. I became more aware of Eva's presence in politics during the 2012 presidential election when she was on television speaking at the Democratic National Convention about being a Latina and getting the votes out in the Latino community. I think it's great when someone in Hollywood uses their celebrity to advocate for good causes. But Eva is about so much more than just putting her name on something. She follows up by making sure she knows everything about the topic. For example, Eva is genuinely interested in Chicano studies and recently received her master's degree in it. She has always loved learning and education and didn't let her career or busy schedule get in the way of achieving her goal to earn her master's—even if it was a little later in life than she had originally planned. Eva was able to go back to school and finally become the student she had always wanted to be. She was eager, excited, and involved in her pursuit of higher learning because she is so passionate about the subject.

I really love how confident Eva is, especially when it comes to how other people see her. For most of her life she has battled a stereotype of being too sexy to be smart, when in fact she is brilliant and a true hustler. I found it refreshing to hear someone as successful as Eva talk about not letting anyone else but herself define who she is. So often people can get caught up in what others think and forget how important it is to believe in who they are. Eva always had the hunger to be successful and the drive to push herself to be the best at everything she does.

Although Eva's career was headed in the direction

of becoming a professional fitness trainer and kinesi-
ologist, her story is a reminder that the best-laid plans
can change in the blink of an eye. She developed her
hunger to better herself by nurturing her need to constantly grow and learn, exploring her personal interest
in helping others, and seeking answers to help advocate
change. After years of being a successful actress, Eva has
become the person she wanted to be by putting her
passion for philanthropy and her community to good
use. She is an inspiration and a role model who is living
proof that it's never too late to follow your passion and
go back to school.

I've always been big on getting a good education. I come
from a family of educators where the pursuit of higher
learning was a part of how I grew up. When I was a student at Texas A&M, I was too young to know how to get
the most out of that experience. Looking back, I didn't
delve deep enough into my major, and I didn't find myself
completely fulfilled by the time I graduated. I studied kinesiology because I love sports and the mechanics of the
body. I wanted to become a trainer on a sports team and
had my eye on working for the Dallas Cowboys. Throughout college, I worked as an aerobics instructor and personal
trainer. I was also a gymnast, cheerleader, and a track run-
ner and competed in beauty pageants. You might say I was

a workout-aholic! I wasn't into living a sedentary lifestyle. It wasn't until my last semester of school that things really got interesting and relevant toward my goal. I registered for graduate school with the hope of getting my master's degree in exercise science. I was dating my college sweetheart and we were all set to get married and go to grad school together. My plan was set, and I felt good about the direction of my future.

I had about a month off between graduating and starting graduate school. I never had a summer where I didn't work or take classes at school. I planned a trip to Los Angeles, where I was scheduled to compete in a modeling and talent competition. I had been named Miss Corpus Christi in 1998 and wanted to keep competing in other pageants. Throughout college, I hadn't allowed myself to take any real vacation time, and I had never been outside Texas, so I was really looking forward to that trip. I immediately fell in love with L.A. I loved the people, the weather, and the beach.

The modeling and talent competition was a weeklong event. My plan was to take part in that and then explore California for a week or two. Much to my surprise, I won the competition. Managers and agents were asking me to sign contracts with them for representation. I had no idea what was happening or the opportunity that was in front of me. I knew I had my bachelor's degree and I could get a job anywhere. "Why not L.A.?" I thought. I found some other struggling actors to share an apartment and then called my mother and asked her to ship my things to

California. At first, she was a little surprised by my plan. It wasn't the idea of me staying in California so much as the fact that I won the pageant. She found it astonishing. At the time, my parents didn't think I was *that* pretty. When I told them I wanted to become an actor, they were very happy as long as I kept my identity and didn't lose myself in the fast-paced Hollywood lifestyle. My parents never spoiled me with riches, but they certainly allowed me to follow my dreams, offering their unwavering love and support. They raised me with a strong sense of self and the belief that I can do anything. Fame was never my goal, but it is the by-product of doing something really well. I promised myself that if I chose to go down this path, I would aim to be the very best.

I didn't give up on the idea of going to graduate school, but I had to give acting a fair try or I would regret it for the rest of my life. In my heart, I knew I would eventually go back to get my master's. I just didn't know when.

As I pursued acting, I knew I needed to find a job to bring in some income. I went to a temp agency looking for work, and they ended up hiring me to be a recruiter. I loved the structure and the idea of working in corporate America. I had a quota of placements to make every month, which I had to either meet or exceed. Anything else would be considered a failure. This high expectation made me accountable and motivated me to make sure I hit my numbers every single month. Failure wasn't something I was very good at, but I am also a realist who likes to manage risk and success. I like barometers of success. I have always enjoyed being measured on my performance, whether it was getting good grades in college or meeting my quota.

When it came to acting, I was always setting goals for myself as a way to measure where I was and whether pursuing acting was the right decision for me. I struggled for a while in L.A., doing "extra" work in films and television. This gave me enough money to pay my bills and rent. Once I accomplished that, I raised the bar for myself and set my next goal—to land a recurring role on a soap opera. My effort paid off and I was eventually cast as Isabella Braña on *The Young and the Restless*, playing that part from 2001 to 2003. Being on a soap was a dream job that I thought would make me happy for the rest of my life. But I didn't stop there. As someone who always wanted to push myself, I set another goal. This time, I wanted to be on a prime-time show as a regular character. I had done some guest-starring roles and a couple of recurring characters on other shows and had a few shows that didn't have a lot of longevity. I wanted to be a part of a hit show where I could spread my wings as an actress and transition from daytime into prime time. My wish came true when I was cast as Gabrielle Solis on *Desperate Housewives* in 2003. I was fortunate enough to play that character until the show wrapped its final season in 2012.

A lot of people thought I was an overnight sensation when *Desperate Housewives* became a hit television series. Little did they know that I had been working consistently for ten years before being cast as Gabrielle. I always had a drive and passion to do well at whatever I set my mind to as I worked my way up through the business. If I was cast as an extra with a walk-on instead of being given a line or two, I was committed to being the best extra on the set. If I had a line to deliver, rest assured, I nailed it like no one else could.

Throughout my years working and paying my dues, I remained humble and grounded and didn't let fame go to my head. People in Hollywood are often defined by what a magazine writes because that is what many consider to be the truth. I never wanted to fall into that trap. I know who I am and would never let anyone tell me otherwise. I'm secure in my identity and love the person I have grown into. From the beginning of my acting career throughout my years working in Hollywood, I've remained true to who I am. I was lucky to come into fame later in life because I already knew who I was as a person.

Although I have no regrets about the time I put into developing my career as an actress, I never had a passion for acting. I just stumbled into it. I love acting and enjoy the process, but I definitely had higher aspirations to continue studying and to discover my real life passion and purpose. I remember someone in college once saying to me, "Someday you are going to have a voice, so you better have something to say." I was thirty-five years old when I realized that I wanted to become a political activist for the Latino community. Early on, I was fortunate enough to give speeches on behalf of the Chavez Foundation and other organizations that assist farmworkers and the UFW (United Farm Workers of America). After I talked about all of the issues that Chicano workers faced in the fields, after my speech, I'd ask, "Is that true?" I couldn't understand why children were dying in fields where they were working and why farmers weren't given water. I felt so out of touch with the real issues the community was facing and wanted to educate myself and be literate on subjects I was advocating for. If I was going to be effective in the work, I needed to become an expert on the history of the Latino community, whether it was immigration history or the political history of Latinos in the United States. I also needed to have a better understanding of how our government works and how policies are created and implemented. I wanted to know every aspect of information so I could fulfill my greatest passion of advocating for the Latino community, so I enrolled in graduate school to get my master's degree in Chicano studies.

Going to graduate school has been one of the great learning experiences of my life. I am a firm believer that it is never too late to go back to school. I may have been the oldest person in my class, but my enthusiasm is as strong as ever. In fact, I'm sure it sometimes annoyed some of my classmates when I repeatedly raised my hand to ask a question! I really enjoyed the classes I took and relearning American history. I spent downtime on the set of *Desperate Housewives* talking about World War I or debating whether the New Deal was a good deal. As a result of getting my master's degree I now understand how and why the world works the way it does. This opening of my mind has shaped my opinion and point of view of the world and has

helped me see how I can do something to make a difference. I strongly believe that if you are Mexican American,
you should take time to study Chicano history. My studies
helped me become more familiar with the needs of our
community.

My pursuit of becoming a political activist was challenging on many levels, but mostly because people didn't
take me seriously at first. I had to go against the image of
who people think I am versus who I really am because of
the character I played on *Desperate Housewives*. Gabrielle
was a sexy, sultry, calculating woman. I will take the sexy
description all day long, but please don't assume that a person cannot be sexy and intelligent. I have encountered this
kind of stereotyping for years. There is a social construct
of what society says women should be, and we need to
overcome it. As an actor, you are not allowed to have an
opinion on anything. The general theory is, "Shut up and
act." When you have something relevant to say, combating
this mentality is an uphill climb.

I understand the challenge most of you face, having
to hustle to find a job today. It's important to know that in
today's world, a college degree does not guarantee that you
will graduate and find a nice six-figure job. You have to go
out and search for opportunities and then figure out a way
into the position. Your degree is just a stepping-stone to
launch your career. Even if you have to accept an internship or a position at the bottom, do it. Start somewhere and
be willing to work your way up. Your education didn't stop
when you graduated. This is when the real work begins.

Sometimes I think people try to follow their passion too soon and let perfection prevent progress. There is a tendency to get caught up in seeking the perfect job that you can be completely passionate about. The focus right out of college should be on getting some experience in learning to fail, fall down, and get back up again. This is the time in your life where you are allowed the freedom to make mistakes and gain invaluable insight from the experience. Trial and error is the best way to determine what avenue is right for you. Spend a little time figuring out your path, and don't settle for something that doesn't feel like a good fit.

John Legend

"Fear of failure stops too many people from doing things. It's not wrong to be afraid, but you have to fight through fear to overcome it."

COLLEGE ATTENDED: University of Pennsylvania, bachelor's degree in English with an emphasis on African American literature

OCCUPATION: Singer, songwriter, actor

John Legend is a person in the entertainment/music industry who stands out to me. He is hugely successful and musically talented but also has the "cool factor" that grabs the attention of people my age.

I always knew John Legend was incredibly gifted musically, but I had no idea he had paid his own way through college, racking up tons of student loans he'd have to deal with after graduating. He got a job right after graduation working at a management consulting group and was persistent throughout all of this to follow his dream of being a musician—and I knew that people would love to hear his story.

He has gone down a few different career paths, even getting involved in politics and making the world a better place, but never lost sight of what he wanted to accomplish in the big picture. John is a great example of someone who trusted his gut, took chances, and worked his butt off to follow his dreams, never giving up one ounce of faith along the way.

Music has been a big part of my life in every phase, from childhood through the present. When I was in college, I was in an a cappella group and directed my church choir every Sunday. I also directed a few theater productions and the school show choir, which was our version of *Glee*. I was always writing my own material and performing in talent shows. I wanted to be a big star—I'd dreamed of being one since I was a little kid. I didn't know what steps to take to get there, but I had that fire in my belly.

Sometimes creative people think they will be discovered and someone will come along and shape them into a star. For a while, that was my plan. But the more I talked to people who understood the music business, I realized that the only way to be heard was to put together a demo with music I'd written that was produced by the right people. I started pulling that together around 1998, during my junior year of college. I was recording with a few different producers and co-writers who wanted to help me launch as a solo artist, but that didn't start to happen until my senior year. I felt like I didn't have a real plan as I neared graduation. I wasn't sure what I really wanted to do. The biggest part of me was gravitating toward my music, so in my mind, whatever else I'd end up doing would only be temporary.

By the time I graduated in 1999, I still hadn't done anything big in music to speak of. After watching all of my friends who were business-centric and influenced by seeing our Wharton School of Business classmates go to work in consulting and banking, I gave in to the peer pressure and decided to join them. The financial sector was a good place to learn a lot about business and get paid a good amount of money. It was like going to graduate school because it could help launch you into whatever else you might want to do afterward. I didn't have any financial support from my parents, and I had student loans to pay back.

I couldn't afford to live in any major urban area unless I had a real job, so I did the résumé drops and interviews that my friends were doing. I was definitely attracted to the job of consulting. It seemed like an interesting career where I could work with the kind of people I liked being around. I interviewed with all of the big firms and finally accepted an offer to work at the Boston Consulting Group.

I never expected to stay in that position for three years, but that's exactly what happened. I was positive I'd get a record deal within my first year or two because I was heavily moonlighting at night as a musician. After work, I'd head to the studio and record, or I'd perform live in a club. I tried to get to New York to play as often as I could.

During this time, I met Kanye West and started

working with him. I would go to the studio in my business casual clothes straight from work. I definitely stood out from the way most of the other people in the studio were dressed. By the time 2002 rolled around, I had a manager who was a pretty high-powered guy named David Sonnenberg. Between David, Kanye, and my lawyer, who was also well connected, I felt like I was close to getting a record deal. There was a buzz around my live performances, and my demos were getting some attention from the right people in the business.

At the three-year mark of working at the Boston Consulting Group, you either decide to stay on track and go to business school or leave. I decided it was time to go. I quit my day job and got a part-time job working at a nonprofit so I could spend more time and energy focused on my music. I struggled for a while, living on my credit cards and skating by because I wasn't making the kind of money I was when consulting. But things happened soon enough because I started touring with Kanye and making money doing sessions for him and other artists. In late 2002 or early 2003, I signed with Kanye's production company. By 2004, I had my first deal with a major label, Columbia Records, and when that happened, I didn't need to worry about money anymore.

As soon as I got my record deal, I took the first check I received and paid off all of my credit card debt and my student loans. No one ever told me about college loan debt or how to manage it. All I knew was that I had to pay that bill as soon as it came in the mail. No one coached me on preparing for my career. I certainly could have used it because I was a little more haphazard than most kids should be. These days, I think it's difficult for kids coming right out of college. The job market isn't as welcoming as it was when I graduated, which is unfortunate timing. The unemployment rate is a lot higher than when I graduated, and kids are getting paid less for the fewer jobs that are available. If things aren't going the way you hoped in your job search, you can't take all of the blame. However, there are ways you can do better and be smarter about your career.

Some careers sound sexier than others, and some are going to sound more fun. It's important to get to know people in the field you want to work in so you can understand what they do and whether you would be a good fit. If you're coming from a place where you're operating without enough information and understanding of what's right for you, you will flounder for a while. You have to be open-minded and willing to learn and then foster that hunger and desire to keep learning. Education doesn't end when you graduate from college. Be open when opportunities present themselves, especially when it comes to meeting people and learning from them. Pay attention to what is happening in the world, read often, and continue to better yourself every day.

I wasn't particularly interested in politics when I was in college and didn't spend a lot of time and energy thinking about it, but I have gotten politically involved since then. It's not because I studied it in school but because I decided it was important to me to start reading a lot about our political system and paying attention to what is happening. I realize that what happens in the world affects me, and my participation in a cause can have an impact. But at the end of the day, my interest in politics won't define who I am—my music will define my legacy and what people think of me. Musicians' songs are recorded impressions of moments of where we once were in our lives. And those songs will always be a part of our legacy when we die. If I hadn't followed my dream to become a full-time musician, I am not sure I would have lived the same fulfilling life. I was willing to risk everything—and wasn't afraid to fail. You learn so much from taking chances, whether they work out or not. Either way, you can grow from the experience and become stronger and smarter.

Sara Blakely

"There is a hidden blessing in the most traumatic things we go through in our lives. My brain always goes to, 'Where is the hidden blessing? What is my gift?'"

COLLEGE ATTENDED: Florida State University, bachelor's degree in communications

OCCUPATION: Founder of Spanx

Almost every person I spoke to focused on the importance of failure in creating their success. In our culture, we grow up thinking that failure is a terrible thing, that it's a setback, or worse, the end. Often it turns out to be the beginning of something better.

When I first discovered Spanx, my initial reaction was, "What a genius idea! Why didn't I think of that?" I thought the product was amazing and a life changer for most women. When I read about Sara and her journey to the success of her company, it inspired me even more, and I knew I had to interview her for this book. She got her start selling fax machines door-to-door—something most of us would absolutely dread doing. To me, convincing people of why that fax machine is right for them sounds like one of the hardest jobs I've ever heard of, and I understood what it was like knocking on random people's doors. I was really young the first time I canvassed door-to-door. I walked around neighborhoods with my cousins, handing out pamphlets and buttons asking people to vote for my uncle, who was running for Congress in Washington. When going door-to-door, you don't really know what you are going to encounter. Sometimes you deal with someone who is upset or disagrees with you, and as a child, that kind of response was scary. It's hard not to get discouraged when people say no or tell you that you are wrong or they don't agree with you, but that never seemed to faze Sara.

As impressed as I was before our interview, I was even more captivated with Sara after we had the chance to speak. She took postponing reality to a new level by choosing to take a job at Disney World right after college in the pursuit of happiness. When that didn't work out as she had hoped, she found herself in sales—pitching a product she didn't love but making a living and choosing to be the best in her field. Sara's story shows the importance of recognizing that you may not have the perfect job right out of college, or even a few years out of college, but there is always something positive to gain from the experience. Throughout her seven-year career selling fax machines, she asked herself some critical questions along the way, such as, "What is the hidden blessing here and what am I supposed to be learning from this?" In Sara's case, hearing "No" every day gave her the ability to become hugely successful because she believed in herself, her product, and her customers.

When people told her the idea to start Spanx was terrible and wouldn't work, she didn't listen. The feeling of rejection was all too familiar, and she knew exactly how to deal with it. Hearing "No" didn't stop her from getting her brilliant idea off the kitchen table and into stores all over the world. It inspired her to succeed—eventually creating a billion-dollar business doing something she loves.

Becoming a lawyer was a rite of passage in my family. My father was a trial attorney. I had been watching him in court since I was eight years old, and I liked the law. When I was a child, my father used to encourage my brother and me to fail. At the dinner table, instead of asking about the best part of our day, he would ask us what we failed at that week. If we didn't have something to tell him, he would be disappointed. When we shared whatever failure we'd endured, he'd high-five us and say, "Way to go!" The gift my father gave us by doing this was redefining what failure truly meant. For me, failure is not the outcome—it is about trying new things, whether I was good at them or not. His pride in our failed attempts made my brother and me want to push ourselves harder. It shook things up for us along the way, but at least we learned what we were good at (and not so good at) early in our lives. After a few of those failed attempts, I learned that something positive always came from the experience.

By the time I got to my senior year of college, it was pretty definitive that I would apply to law school and head in that direction after graduation. I took the LSAT twice, and both times I didn't get the scores I needed to get into law school. By graduation day, my plan wasn't exactly in the place I had expected it to be. I was pretty traumatized in wondering what I was going to do with my life, because law school was not in my future. I vividly remember walking across the stage on graduation day to receive my diploma thinking, "What now?"

I had dedicated the past fifteen years of my life to school, participating in debate clubs in high school and college and watching my dad excel as a lawyer, believing this would be my path too. It was shocking to realize this wasn't going to be my life. I was so devastated that I hadn't done well on my LSAT that I wanted to escape reality a little longer after college before figuring out what I would do. So I came up with a plan B. I would get into my car and drive from where I grew up in Clearwater Beach, Florida, to Disney World in Orlando and try out to play the character Goofy. Something about being Goofy felt right—comfortable and at least no one would know it was me inside that costume. It turns out that you have to be at least five feet, eight inches tall to be Goofy—two inches taller than I am. It was an all-time low point for me when I discovered that I wasn't even qualified to be Goofy!

They said I could be a chipmunk—three months after I started. Disney World has a policy that you can't become a character until you've worked at the park for a minimum of three months, as a way to prevent people from bouncing around too much. I spent three months passing the time at Disney World wearing a brown polyester space suit putting people on rides at Epcot at the World of Motion and working on the moving sidewalk for eight hours a day. I stuck it out for the three months, but it sure was humbling. I had people I knew from college show up and find me wearing big Mickey Mouse ears and a name tag that boldly read "Sara Blakely." They couldn't hide their surprise or curiosity about whether I had graduated.

"Is that really you?" they'd ask.

"Yes, it is. Now get on the ride," I said.

Disney is a fabulous corporation, and it was cool to be behind the scenes while learning about the Disney culture. Working at Disney World was a pleasant enough experience for the few months I was there, but the truth is I was bored. And I was unhappy. There were plenty of times on the moving sidewalk when tears would stream down my face without my realizing it. This was my life . . . and, as it turns out, Disney World was not the happiest place on earth for me. There was nothing real about going on a break and seeing Snow White dragging on a cigarette. My attempt to escape reality by going to Disney World backfired, and in the end, I never did get the chance to be one of the characters. That was when I knew it was time to face the real world.

I moved back home to live with my mom and accepted a job with an office supply company selling fax machines door-to-door. For me, moving home was a great way to save some money while I launched my new career in sales. Plus, I get along really well with my mom, so it was a supportive and harmonious environment. The company I went to work for didn't offer a lot of training. They gave me a copy of the phone book and four zip codes to work in and said I needed to sell $20,000 a month to make it in their company. No leads were provided. It was straight-up cold-calling on businesses. There were also no repeat customers because once I sold a machine, they usually didn't need another. I'd get into my car at eight a.m. and drive to various office parks until five p.m. five days a week. I walked into the offices unannounced and did my best to sell them a fax machine. It turned out I had a knack for selling and became quite successful within the organization. By the time I was twenty-five years old, I had been promoted to national sales trainer for the company, doing seminars around the country teaching people how to sell door-to-door.

Selling fax machines was humbling and, though I didn't realize it at the time, a tremendous training ground for dealing with rejection. I look back on that time in my life as being such a big part of the success of Spanx, the company I would go on to found seven years later. All I heard was "No" from sunup to sundown. People ripped up my business card in my face at least once or twice a week. Sometimes I was escorted out of the buildings by security guards. And despite all of that, I still found a way to remain positive and keep knocking on doors. Ultimately, I realized that being successful in sales is a numbers game. Eventually, someone would need what I was selling, and when they showed their interest, I knew how to close the deal.

Three events in my early life shaped my fierce persistence and perseverance. First, my father left my mother when I was sixteen years old. Just before he moved out, he came into my bedroom and handed me a motivational tape series by Dr. Wayne Dyer called *How to Be a No-Limit Person*. He said, "I wish I had discovered this when I was your age instead of waiting until the age of forty to learn this information." That statement left an indelible mark, so I listened to the series over and over until I had all ten tapes memorized. The primary message was about the power of visualization, the law of attraction, and how to think in a way that makes you the most productive person you can be without worrying what other people think.

The second impactful event on my life was learning to debate in high school. If you master the artful skill of debating, it teaches you to see both sides of an issue and how to think critically and quickly on your feet. Learning these techniques early in life helped me become fearless in sales and taught me to see "No" not as an ending but as an opportunity to turn it into "Yes."

The third was learning to cold-call on businesses. It took some practice, but I found a way to walk into an office without an appointment and confidently sell them my product by selling myself. If someone said "No," over time, I learned that I could get at least fifteen more seconds of time and use it to go from a slamming door to a sale. Cold-calling taught me a lot about using humor, making people laugh, and the power of a big smile. I even tried doing stand-up comedy for a while at night as a way to sharpen my wit and humor. Although standup wasn't really for me, I assure you that I got more results using those three techniques than any others I tried over the years.

I spent seven years selling fax machines, and all the while, I was dreaming about finding a product of my own that I could sell. I spent endless hours analyzing my strengths and weaknesses and how to take what I knew and make it work for me in a different way. I didn't enjoy selling fax machines, but I liked dealing with people and selling them something they needed—even if they didn't know it yet. I wanted to create my own product that I could sell to millions of people who believed in it as much as I did. That became my mantra. I wrote it in my journal every day. Having a mental snapshot of where you are, where you are going, and what you are moving toward is incredibly powerful.

When I came up with the idea to start Spanx, I had never taken a business class or worked in fashion or retail. I grew up on a beach where everyone wears cutoff shorts, flip-flops, and bathing suits eleven months of the year. High fashion and design were foreign to me. The office supply company I worked for transferred me to Atlanta, where I noticed everyone dressed up, whether they were working in offices or the women shopping or having lunch with their friends. All of the women looked so cute, wearing pretty colorful dresses or little capri pants and high heels. I wanted to look like I fit in, so I purchased a pair of cream-colored capri pants that hung in my closet for eight months. Every time I put them on, I felt like I needed to wear a thong to pull them off, and even that didn't make me feel good in them. Although I was a size two, I had some cellulite on the back of my thighs that you could see through the pants. I was terribly frustrated by not having the right undergarment available so I could wear those pants with comfort and confidence. I went back to the store where I bought the pants and asked the saleswoman what I should wear under the pants that would make my legs look smooth. She directed me to the shapewear department. Being young and in relatively good shape, I had never heard of shapewear before, let alone worn it. When I put on the leggings they suggested, they were so thick, it felt like I was wearing workout clothes. Plus they were far more firming and provided more control than I actually needed, which made them extremely uncomfortable. Worse, I could see a big bulge in my thigh from where the shaper stopped down my leg. Those leggings weren't solving my issue. If anything, it made things worse. So you might say I started Spanx out of necessity and as a frustrated consumer.

I had an idea.

I went home and cut the feet off of my control top panty hose and put them on to see if they would do the trick. It worked perfectly, except the bottom of the stockings rolled up my legs all night. Still, my butt and legs looked firm and smooth. I went home later that night trying to figure out a way to keep the bottom of the stockings comfortable below the knee. I knew it would make a huge difference in a lot of women's lives if I could solve this dilemma.

I wasn't the first woman to cut the feet off of my panty hose and wear them as a body shaper. But I had been visualizing a different life for myself the whole time I was selling fax machines. I had been asking the universe for an idea I could see and writing in my journal that I wanted this idea to manifest in my life. These were all techniques I learned from listening to Wayne Dyer for so many years. The idea and opportunity I had been asking for was right before my eyes.

I began looking up hosiery manufacturers on the Internet to pitch them my idea. Every single company I called told me no. I knew from my cold-calling experience that face-to-face meetings are so much better than phone calls, so I took a week off work and drove around North Carolina, where most shapewear is made in the United States, and met with different companies to share my invention. I went from one hosiery mill to the next, begging each man (yes, men) to make my product. They all said no. Naturally, they couldn't understand what I was selling and why it was innovative. In the meantime, I also looked for patent attorneys in Atlanta who might be willing to help me patent my product. I met with three different firms that each asked for three to five thousand dollars to write my patent. I had five thousand dollars set aside in savings from selling fax machines, but I didn't want to blow it all on paying a lawyer. So I went to Barnes & Noble, found a book on trademarks and patents, and wrote my own patent. I persuaded a lawyer to write the claims over a weekend for a discounted fee, because they are the most important legal part of a patent filing, and I wasn't secure that I could pull that off myself.

I came up with the name Spanx while sitting in typical Atlanta bumper-to-bumper traffic—which gave me lots of time to scribble down every thought that came to my mind behind the wheel of my car, all the while still selling fax machines. I wanted the name to be slightly funny, naughty, uncomfortable, and pressworthy. After work, I developed the packaging at the house of a friend who had just finished graphic design school. I had a clear vision of what I wanted the package to look like, and she transferred my thoughts into what became my actual packaging.

When I had the final package and product finished, I decided to send a gift basket to Oprah Winfrey with a note. Much to my surprise, she chose it as one of her favorite products of the year in her annual "Oprah's favorite things" episode. At the time, my product was in only two stores. After I got those orders, I left home and basically stood in department stores selling Spanx, ensuring its success for the next two years.

When I look back on my college education, I am grateful for the path my life took. If I hadn't bombed out on the LSAT exam, I would never have redirected my life to come up with Spanx. Failures are life's way of nudging you and letting you know you are off course. Trying new things and not being afraid to fail along the way are more important than what you learn in school. The way we process and think is far more important than specifics taught in a classroom. My success came from pushing myself out of my comfort zone and being willing to fail without feeling bad about the outcome. Eventually, all of that hard work and rejection paid off.

Blake Mycoskie

"What got us to where we are today is not going to get us to where we need to go tomorrow."

COLLEGE ATTENDED: Southern Methodist University
OCCUPATION: Founder and Chief Shoe Giver, TOMS Shoes

I was lucky to grow up with parents who believe that it is important for us to see the world. I have been going on eye-opening trips my entire life, whether it was volunteering for the Special Olympics or visiting orphanages in Africa when I traveled on behalf of ONE. Walking around a slum in a third world country quickly puts into perspective what really matters in life. It grounds you in a way that you can't experience without getting out of your bubble at home. The simplest things we take for granted, such as clean drinking water and indoor plumbing, don't exist in many places. I will never forget seeing children in Kenya running around and playing in an open sewer, exposed to great health risks, and yet, despite having nothing, they were happy and appreciative for what they did have. Seeing those smiling faces made me especially appreciative for all that I have been blessed with in my life and always made me come home with a better sense of what really matters and not taking things for granted.

I remember first hearing about TOMS Shoes in high school and rushing out to buy a pair because I thought the concept for his company was so great. I wanted to interview Blake Mycoskie because I admired that he created such a successful company with such a simple idea. Blake's concept was so basic, yet no one had successfully built a One for One model the way he did until he launched TOMS Shoes. I don't know that a lot of people would have taken a trip to Argentina and realized the children had no shoes, like Blake did, and decided to take that into their own hands to do something about it. I was curious to know more about a man who could open his eyes to something so real and needed, and actually follow through to make it happen.

Even though Blake dropped out of college after two years, he had an entrepreneurial mind-set. If something doesn't exist, that doesn't mean it can't exist. It just doesn't exist because nobody has had the courage to follow through on the idea.

After speaking with Blake, I knew his message would resonate with many of us coming out of college, trying to figure it all out. Even though he is a bit older than we are and stayed in college for only two years, I think of him as the first generation of a role model we can point to and say, "I like what he did. I want to do something like that." A lot of kids in my generation want to create a niche product for the marketplace.

They realize something doesn't exist and then create it. My parents' generation didn't have those same opportunities, as most of their peers took a more traditional path. The entrepreneurial experience is really what I think the job market needs today, and that mind-set is what I think defines our generation.

While attending SMU at age nineteen, I started my first company. It was a door-to-door laundry business called EZ Laundry that really took off. Eventually, I was so busy doing other people's laundry that I didn't have time to go to school. I fell in love with the entrepreneurial experience and decided to focus my time on business instead of studying. I don't think college is for everyone. School is awesome, but for me, I was learning a lot more outside the classroom in the real world than I was in school. My parents supported my decision because they could see how excited and passionate I was about the laundry business. I am sure they were nervous because they both have college degrees. They trusted me, believing that if I was passionate about something, it would be a good learning experience. I had enough revenue coming in from the laundry business to support myself, but it was good to know that if everything fell apart, I could still go back to my parents' house and always have a place to sleep.

Ten years after I dropped out of college, having started three other businesses—Mycoskie Media, an outdoor advertising company; Drivers Ed Direct, an online driver's education company; and Reality Central, a television network—and having been on *The Amazing Race*, I realized I had a talent for creating companies. I didn't have the fear that a lot of people have when they're trying to launch an idea. My whole philosophy was to be an entrepreneur and make as much money as possible so that when I was in my fifties and sixties, I could retire and spend my life giving it all away. My idea was always based on giving back, but I didn't think you could make money *and* give it all away at the same time. That was the birth of becoming what I call a "social entrepreneur."

While vacationing in Argentina in 2006, I spent a day volunteering with a local nonprofit delivering used shoes to children in the villages outside Buenos Aires. I had never really done any kind of charity work like that before, and I couldn't believe that kids needed shoes to go to school and didn't have them. That seemed like such an easy thing to provide. So I went with these women to a village and saw kids and families who were so excited to get these shoes— and they weren't even new shoes! They were used shoes. And it just hit me right in the heart. This was what I wanted to be doing. I mean, business is great. Making money's fun, but making people have tears of joy? That's what life's about.

My epiphany moment to start TOMS came when I realized that I could start a for-profit business, not a charity, to continually give new shoes to children in need. I would sell an updated version of the alpargata, a canvas slipper I saw people wearing all over Argentina. Although the ones

I saw people wearing weren't made very well, I was positive I could make some improvements and sell them in the United States.

When I returned from my trip to Argentina, I started with 250 shoes. It wasn't a big undertaking. I created the One for One business model, which provides a new pair of TOMS shoes to a child in need for every pair purchased. Today, we have given more than ten million pairs of new shoes around the world. I originally called the company Shoes for Tomorrow, but later I shortened the name to TOMS Shoes. We've since gone on to create TOMS Eyewear using the One for One model. For every pair of glasses sold, people in need receive prescription glasses, sight-saving surgery, or medical treatment.

To make it in the real world, you have to be willing to experiment and try new things. Whatever you're going to do, do it really well and do it small, and if you're successful there, business will come. Start small, focus, get it right, and then let the growth come. What got us to where we are today is not going to get us to where we need to go tomorrow. You have to question things and look at new opportunities. If I hadn't taken that trip to Argentina, I am not sure I would have started TOMS Shoes. Of course, this awakening came ten years after I left college, but I am a big believer in the value of traveling while you are young. The experiences you have in other countries can inspire greatness. I also think it is important not to jump into the first job you're offered. Take time to look at and weigh all of your opportunities. It's not a perfect science. If you're in a job you're not passionate about, get out of it. Don't get stuck doing something that you are not excited to be a part of.

I was lucky to find my passion for starting businesses at such an early age, and even luckier to refine that passion into coming up with creative solutions to solve the world's problems. It is the process of creation and community building that I love the most. Building TOMS has been immensely rewarding because our business model allows everyone to be a philanthropist or to do a charitable act through the simple purchase of a pair of shoes or eyewear. That alone is the most defining thing I have done as a businessman and in my career so far. The One for One model was a revolutionary idea that many companies are now incorporating into their business. We did it first and made it mainstream, and I am extremely proud of that. The simplicity of the model is what made the company so huge. You buy a pair of shoes and we give a pair of shoes. It's easy to understand and no funky accounting.

So often, people take a job because it pays well. This scenario enables you to have a lifestyle that is supported by that money, and therefore, you find yourself stuck in that job for the rest of your life. You become a slave to the money, working to keep up with the lifestyle you've grown accustomed to instead of enjoying the moment. When you grow dependent on money, you won't get to follow your passion. This is why I always advise people never to take a job for the money—especially when you are young and just starting out. Passion breeds excellence. When you are good at something, the money always follows.

Jennifer Meyer

"What's better than blowing money on your dream?"

COLLEGE ATTENDED: Syracuse University, bachelor's degree in family and child psychology

OCCUPATION: Jewelry designer, entrepreneur

Jennifer Meyer's entrepreneurial spirit is something I really admire. Although there is an age difference between us, I have always looked up to her for her artistic accomplishments and great sense of style. Jennifer was inspired to start designing jewelry after her grandmother taught her the basics of making enamel jewelry when she was a little girl. When she first launched her jewelry line at Barney's New York department stores, I was an immediate fan. Her first design was her trademark piece of jewelry, an eighteen-karat-gold leaf charm, which symbolized "turning over a new leaf." A mutual friend of ours gave me a wishbone necklace designed by Jennifer for my birthday, and I have been obsessed ever since. I am not alone, because she was awarded the prestigious CFDA Award in 2013 for her work.

Jennifer is one of the most humble and down-to-earth women I have met. Although I think her work is pure genius, what I think makes her so successful is her passion for what she does. She works hard and has built her company from the ground up on her own. Her road to success wasn't as easy as you might think. Although Jennifer comes from a family that could have easily provided her with opportunities by opening doors, her parents chose to let her find her own way, which I think is admirable. Parents can be enablers with their kids, often paving the way to take the easy road instead of the more difficult one.

Jennifer's father didn't give her the option to fail or fall into that all-too-common trap. His decision not to offer continued financial support, one of the hardest decisions a parent can make, set his daughter on the right course. By Jennifer's own admission, it was the best thing he could have done for her and was the awakening she needed to understand that real life starts the moment you hold that diploma in your hand. I am awed by her resilience, creativity, and willingness to go out there and discover her passion by working in various jobs that brought her to her dream. It takes courage and a strong sense of self-assuredness to tackle the unknown with such dignity and grace.

Three weeks after I graduated from college I got a call from my dad asking me what my plan was. I had no idea what he was talking about, mostly because I didn't have a plan other than taking some time off and figuring things out. When I gave him that response, he said, "Great idea. How do you plan to support yourself and live if you are taking time off and don't have a job?" I was stunned. "I thought maybe you might help me?" I said. This answer didn't go over as well as I had hoped. It's not that I didn't want to work. I had been working summer jobs since I was fourteen years old. I always had a job to make a little bit of cash on my own. But when I graduated from college, I thought it might be okay for me to take a little break. I was wrong. Real life started the moment I held that diploma in my hand.

My father made it clear that I could take three weeks and do whatever I wanted to do. Then I had to find a job within two weeks—any job. He didn't care where I worked as long as I wasn't sitting at home doing nothing. If I didn't comply, he assured me that I could live at his home for as long as I wanted without paying rent or buying my own groceries, but he would not give me a dime for anything else.

"Your friends are going to get sick of having to pay for you all of the time because you'll have no money of your own. You won't be able to buy gas for your car, go out to eat, or see a movie," he said.

I didn't know what else to do but cry. I was a twenty-one-year-old girl who didn't understand where this sudden but clear ultimatum was coming from. Looking back, it could have been worse. He could have told me I had to move out and live on my own—something I wasn't prepared for at all. In many ways, I was lucky because the pressure to find a job in two weeks was about all I could handle in that moment.

Though I didn't know it then, my father's actions became the biggest eye-opening experience of my life. I didn't have time to sulk. I knew my dad meant every word he said, so I needed to take action—and fast. I called a friend who owned a PR company and told her I was in trouble—that I needed to find a job. She was on her way to the Toronto Film Festival and said I could come along as an entry-level assistant for eight days. Though she wasn't paying me a lot of money, I knew it was enough to buy myself another week of searching, so I said yes. During that week, the editor-in-chief of *Glamour* magazine put the word out that they were looking for a new West Coast beauty and fitness editor. I was twenty-one years old and had never written a line of anything worth reading except a few essays I'd written in college. I wasn't a writer, but I always wanted to be in fashion in some way and thought this might be the perfect avenue toward that goal. The job piqued my interest enough to call my dad and ask him to buy me a plane ticket to New York so I could interview for the position. At first, he was resistant, saying, "You have no job and now you are asking me to buy you a plane ticket?" I pleaded and begged until I finally convinced him that I really had a job interview—so he finally gave in and said he'd purchase the ticket.

I went to New York without a clue about what I was supposed to do. I walked into the interview with no résumé and very little practical experience. What I did have was a passion for fashion and an understanding of what people want to read in magazines. I knew what was trending in L.A. and was fairly tuned in to the next great fad long before it went mainstream. Knowing my time was running out, I practically got down on my hands and knees asking for the job—promising that if they hired me, I would do my very best. I left the interview uncertain of my fate. I flew back to L.A. and waited. Much to my surprise, they called to say they wanted to hire me. Getting that phone call with my first real job offer was the best moment I could have ever wished for because it was the beginning of something that would take me toward my ultimate dream.

I discovered at an early age that you can learn something from everyone you meet. You have to keep your eyes and ears open at all times. That was the attitude I had when I started as an editor at *Glamour*. I worked especially hard to make new and solid connections in the fashion world that I could cultivate throughout my career. I knew that if I worked hard and did a good job, one door would lead to another. And it did. Through one of my contacts, I was offered the opportunity to work for Giorgio Armani's public relations department, which was the most amazing and intense learning experience. It was an incredible opportunity to travel to Milan and learn about couture. It was hard work that took a lot of perseverance and a willingness to push my own limits, but it paid off because I suddenly found myself in an amazing position, learning about something in which I had a great interest. I never once thought about how much more I could be making someplace else or how many hours I put in each week. I just did my job. As I got better in my field, I was absolutely certain I wanted to stay involved in fashion.

I left Armani for a new position with Ralph Lauren in New York. It was right around this time that I met my husband, Tobey Maguire. I'd always had the idea of starting my own jewelry line in the back of my brain, but I pretty much wrote it off as a ridiculous dream. Tobey encouraged me to follow my dream, but I had my doubts. I didn't go to school for business or jewelry, didn't know the first thing about how to get started, and had no idea where I would get the money to launch my own line. I didn't want to ask to borrow money from anyone because I didn't know what I was doing. But then one day Tobey said, "I am tired of hearing you talk about it! Just do it!"

I grew up believing there is no "try"—there is only "do." Either you do it or you don't. After giving it a lot of thought, I realized that I had saved enough money to make a couple of pieces. If those were well received, I could figure out the next steps. What's better than blowing money on your dream? I related to jewelry and truly believed that I had a knack for knowing what other people would want to wear.

If you follow your passion, you will reach your dreams. If you are lucky enough to find yourself with an opportunity to do something you are passionate about, and if you're financially able to, you should take a chance and do it.

Bear Grylls

"Life doesn't reward the naturally clever or strong but those who can learn to fight and work hard and never quit."

COLLEGE ATTENDED: Eton College and University of London, bachelor's degree in Spanish and Latin American studies

OCCUPATION: Adventurer, star of *Man vs. Wild*

When thinking of life after college, most of us tend to think about the usual things we will need to be aware of in order to survive: food, rent, money, and so on. Bear Grylls has made a career out of constantly testing the concept of survival.

Bear has always managed to follow his passion. He is a risk taker, and he advises going down the road less traveled to make for a more interesting life experience. He has created a job for himself that consistently keeps him on his toes and always puts him in situations that require him to dig deep and challenge himself in order to come out alive.

College taught me the value of having a few good friends and being prepared to do what you love. Though I wasn't book smart, there was no doubt that I knew my path after college would lead me to joining the Army. My father was a Royal Marine Commando, something I always admired, though I was determined to get one up on him by joining the Special Air Service, also known as the SAS, a special regimen of the British Army. I enjoyed climbing and learning survival skills and thought the Army would help me sharpen those traits.

My dad once told me to follow my core competency and my heart and to never give up. When I joined the Army, I wasn't thinking about doing something extraordinary so much as I was looking to do what I was good at and loved. More so, it gave me the opportunity to embrace a bit of risk and taught me not to get downhearted by failures. Failures teach us more than successes.

Tap into your passion without worrying about money—just follow your dream. Most people struggle with the fear of the unknown, especially after college graduation. What I've learned over the years is that the path less traveled always makes for a more interesting journey. If you simply do what everyone else is doing, how can you ever expect to excel and create something wonderful and unique in your life?

If you can, choose a career that inspires you and does

something that betters other people's lives. You can do this if you learn to listen to and trust your instincts and don't get caught up with keeping a certain image or appearance for the sake of others. Be honest, keep things light and fun, and above all, have a dream that you aren't willing to give up on.

One of my favorite quotes comes from Winston Churchill: "When going through hell, keep going." It has inspired me whenever I've been in tough situations where I've been faced with great challenges and found the courage to push through. All worthwhile journeys have big obstacles. It's the way of the world. The rewards go to those who can push through those trying moments and still manage to keep a smile on their face.

I always enjoy pushing my own boundaries and keeping things fresh by stepping out of my comfort zone. Summiting Mt. Everest and passing SAS selection involved embracing great risk and discomfort, but both helped define my path in life. The lesson is to go to those places where it is hard and make your mark. For me, it isn't so much about my career as it is doing what makes me feel alive—even in the face of death.

My best life lessons and education didn't come from a classroom—they've come from the wild. How you act in the big moments, the ones that challenge you, scare you, tempt you, and force you to make the right decisions, is what defines you. As long as you remain willing to work hard, maintain your integrity, and keep your friends and family close, you will succeed in whatever you choose to do.

Lauren Bush Lauren

"The awesome thing about being young and just starting out is that you don't know the rules yet and it is easier to take a risk and just do things."

COLLEGE ATTENDED: Princeton University, bachelor's degree in anthropology and a certificate in photography

OCCUPATION: Fashion model and designer, founder of "FEED"

I was in high school when I first heard about Lauren Bush's idea for her FEED tote bags as a way to raise awareness and money to feed the hungry. I thought it was the most genius idea to create something so fashionable that raised money for a great cause. I went to Africa in my sophomore year of college and saw the makeshift "maternity wards" in obscure impoverished villages. When I returned I was inspired to design my own FEED bag to raise money for maternal mortality. I admire Lauren's drive and passion, especially her ability to find a way to do something she loved at such a young age that helped others in need and then make it her job.

I am equally impressed by her self-awareness out of college. She started working at a political think tank and realized within a week that it wasn't a good fit. If you know something isn't right for you, there's not a lot of value in staying in that position unless it's strictly for financial reasons. Sometimes, of course, sticking things out has its advantages. When I interned for the documentary unit at CNN, I knew the first day I got there that I had no interest in being in that specific unit. Still, it was an internship, and I knew it wasn't going to be a long-term commitment, so I decided to make the best of the experience and stayed for the duration of the summer. And because I did, I was able to experience other components of CNN and feel a completely different energy from the day-to-day routine that I can only describe as the craziest and coolest energy I have ever experienced. Had I quit after that first week, I would have never been able to experience that firsthand.

So many people view college as the place that sets you up for greater things and prepares you for your next steps—not as a place that sets you up for disappointment or feeling lost and unprepared after you graduate.

Lauren talked openly about her feelings after college and how so many people feel happy and accomplished and then suddenly find themselves deflated and sad when reality sets in and things don't come together as quickly as they might have planned.

$\longleftrightarrow$

In 2005, I traveled to Chad as a student ambassador for the United Nations World Food Programme, where I witnessed firsthand the powerful impact of the lack of food in impoverished countries. I got the idea to start FEED Projects after I took that trip during my junior year of college. FEED is an initiative to fight world hunger on behalf of the World Food Programme. I raised money for the fight by selling burlap bags with the FEED logo on the outside. When I launched FEED Projects, I had never been involved in designing or manufacturing. I had an interest in traveling and learning about different parts of the world and studying their cultures.

Although world hunger is thought of as too over-whelming and too far away for people to engage, I believed in the idea that people want to help feed starving kids around the world. My FEED bag idea was a way for people to connect and realize they were having an impact on world hunger through a consumer purchase. I had tremendous faith that whether FEED worked out or not, something would eventually come together. Having the freedom to dream and think about my future was a gift.

I created a prototype of my first FEED bag, and I knew I wanted to shop it around to specific outlets. I was working closely with the World Food Programme as I tried to make my first sale. I was able to get Amazon interested, but for various reasons, the World Food Programme said they couldn't be the vendor of the bags. Amazon wouldn't buy the bags unless there was an actual vendor. So I decided to go from designer to vendor, creating FEED as a way to close my first order, which fed five hundred children in school for a year.

Starting FEED happened so fast. I graduated in May 2006, and by February 2007 my company was set up and fulfilling orders. It was a crazy time because I was doing odd jobs in between to make ends meet. I had an idea to write for a magazine, got a job at a political think tank, and continued to pursue manufacturing the FEED bags in my spare time. I was lucky that I modeled in high school and throughout college, and had saved enough money to support myself during those first several months. To keep my expenses affordable and to stretch my savings, I lived in a six-floor walk-up on the Lower East Side of Manhattan with friends. We all crammed into that apartment and made the most of it. It was comforting to know that I could pay my rent without having to worry, but I knew I was living off past income. Modeling was always an easy way to make money, but I wanted to do something I enjoyed that would contribute something substantial back to society. It wasn't easy to walk away from the income stream, but I knew it wasn't going to allow me the space and freedom to figure things out, which I needed to do to relieve my post-college anxiety.

When you leave college, you have a great sense of confidence, which can soon be deflated when you realize how hard it is to get a job you love. And if you are lucky enough to land a job right out of school, discovering that you will likely start at the ground level and will have to do menial tasks can be challenging. This false sense of security can set you up for disappointment, but having your college degree helps in the pursuit. It's hard to know what you don't know, especially when you are trying to find your first job. People get nervous and jump on the first opportunity that comes their way. One main purpose of having a job is to support yourself and be independent. At the same time, fear can start you down a track that is not ideal for you. I have seen so many people get their first job and think, "This is it!" Of course, it may not be. It may take three or four jobs to discover your true career path.

It can be paralyzing not to know what your first, second, or third step should be. But once you take those first few steps, things do get easier—even if you're not where you're supposed to be just yet. I don't think that a college degree necessarily equates to success, but it gives you that extra boost to go out there, network, and bolster your chances. And taking chances on opportunities, even if they aren't right for you, gives you a clearer picture of where you want to go with your life and career. Sometimes those negative experiences teach us more than the ones that work out.

There are many different routes to success. I started my own venture, but that didn't necessarily mean I would become successful doing it. You can have a great idea, but if you don't execute it well and have the skill set and knowledge base to make the most of it, then it is not going to work. At the end of the day, a college degree isn't what makes you smart; it's curiosity and the desire to seek answers and practical knowledge to help guide you in your field of choice.

Brad Wollack

*"It's important to find one person
who believes in you."*

COLLEGE ATTENDED: University of Southern California, bachelor's degree in political science and journalism,
MBA

OCCUPATION: Writer, *Chelsea Lately,* and comedian

I wanted to interview Brad Wollack because I am a big
fan of *Chelsea Lately* and love watching him on her show
when he does the round table. I ran into him while I
was on vacation with my family, where I decided to
introduce myself and ask him if he'd be interviewed for
this book. He is hysterically funny and, as I discovered,
exceptionally smart. You don't meet many comedians
and writers who have a master's degree.

I respect that Brad decided to go back to college
to get his MBA when he was stalled getting work as a
writer. His parents supported his decision to pursue his
dream, but they didn't believe he would be able to support himself without something to fall back on. Even
though he was offered a full-time job writing for Chelsea Handler, he continued to go to school to earn his

MBA and work for her at the same time. I admire that kind of dedication and commitment, especially knowing that what he learned in business school is relevant to his career today.

When I first considered attending USC, I applied to their film school, but I didn't get in. It was devastating because I thought I was going to be the next Steven Spielberg. I knew I wanted to be in entertainment somehow, but I didn't know what aspect. I mostly wanted to be in show business to show the girls from high school, well, one in particular whom I had a crush on, that I was right when I told her I was going to be famous someday.

I ended up going to USC anyway, where I studied political science and journalism. I worked at the student TV station, where I did a sports show for USC Trojan Vision. I was mostly doing humorist hosting and correspondent work. I wasn't well versed in it, but I enjoyed doing it. Fox Sports West liked what I was doing enough to use me as the correspondent for their USC show, where I would interview athletes every week.

Two weeks before I graduated, I signed with William Morris, a talent agency in Los Angeles, because Fox was looking for someone to host a pilot sports show. An agent from William Morris actually sought me out, finding me at a friend's final student film screening. When the lights went up, some guy grabbed me and said, "What's your name?" When I told him, he said, "I have been looking for you." It turns out he was a big television agent who had packaged the pilot for Fox. It wasn't what I thought I'd be doing right out of college, but it was an entrée into the business. It would also give me more footage to compile a reel to send out to smaller stations around the country, looking to be the "funny" correspondent on a morning show or the local news.

Uncertain about the financial stability of being in show business and whether the Fox gig would work out, I took a job substitute teaching in South Central L.A. I needed something to pay the bills and still allow me the flexibility to go to meetings and pursue my work in TV. I got my teaching credentials to work in elementary school for grades K–5. If I had worked with kids any bigger, I would have been outsized. I wasn't taking that risk. I didn't want to wait tables because I had done that during the summers in college and knew it wasn't for me. It turns out that substituting was a lot harder than I expected it to be. The kids I was teaching didn't have a lot of positive reinforcement at home. I used to end every class like I was the great white hope. I would give an inspirational speech to second graders who looked at me like they had no idea what I was saying. "You can make it out of here and go to college . . ." type of stuff. About a year in, I knew I'd hit the wall and couldn't do it anymore. I was at school and had just broken up a fight between two third graders in the yard.

What am I doing here? I thought.

I went back to my classroom and wrote the word *pathetic* on the chalkboard.

"Who can tell me what this means?" I asked my class. One kid raised his hand and said, "Not good."

"That's right, and that's what you all are. Pathetic." I said.

In my head, I was thinking, *Are you kidding me?* I was a privileged white kid standing in a classroom in the worst part of L.A. calling these disadvantaged young Latino and African American kids pathetic. I was so pissed at myself. Who did I think I was? What was I thinking? I knew it was time to get out.

That night, I booked my first national commercial and never taught again. I ended up getting a lot of work because I had what casting agents described as a "unique" look. Doing commercial work paid well, but it wasn't challenging enough for me. I was still doing standup and knew I could write funny material. I told my agents I wanted them to submit me for writing jobs. I was still open to going on auditions, but writing comedy felt like a move in the right direction.

The first show I was put up for to work on as a writer was *The Wayne Brady Show*. I wrote up a sample monologue for Wayne, who loved it. Before I knew it, I was sitting in a meeting with Wayne and his manager, Bernie Brillstein. Meeting Wayne was cool, but meeting Bernie, well, he is a legend in television.

I got the gig, but it turned out to be horrible. I was

really young to be writing and everyone else on the staff resented my presence. Even though it was a rough experience and I only lasted half a season, I received a Daytime Emmy nomination for my work. I left *The Wayne Brady Show* on good terms and continued to write and produce for other people, as well as Wayne, for the next three or four years. It's so important to be nice to everyone because you never know when you are going to see or work with them again.

I spent the next few years going from gig to gig. Sure, they were jobs, but everything wasn't really adding up to a career. There were moments when I thought about moving back to Northern California to go into the wine business with my dad, but I am not a quitter and wasn't willing to give up that easily. Something always drove me back to comedy. Nothing fired me up like writing and producing funny bits. I couldn't find passion in anything else.

Although my parents were always supportive of my comedy and writing, they didn't think I would make a career out of it. They believed in me, but I don't think they believed in the entertainment business. I was showing signs of frustration, and they were beginning to nudge me to go back to school. My parents thought it might be a good idea for me to get my MBA. At the time, I felt it was the right thing to do. I applied to business school at USC and got in. It was around this same time that I was hired as a writer for *The Chelsea Handler Show*, a sketch comedy show that preceded what became *Chelsea Lately*. When you do freelance work, you never know how long a project will last. I thought *The Chelsea Handler Show* would be a six-month gig. I was juggling business school at night and writing for the show during the day—something I wouldn't generally recommend. It was challenging, but worth it. Chelsea's show kept getting extended, which meant I would do both because I was so far into getting my MBA. It didn't make sense not to complete it. No one else will believe in you as much as you believe in yourself. And when the days come where you have some doubt, it's important to find that one person who believes in you. A few people along the way took an interest in my career, but they didn't have the vehicle to help me grow. It took me six years after college to find that person who believed in me, despite what anyone else said. Chelsea Handler has been a mentor and advocate in my corner from the day we met. She doesn't care where I came from, who I am, or what I am about. As long as she sees something special in you, she wants you on her team. That unwavering support makes me want to kill for her, and it helped me go from having jobs to finding my career.

Many people will say they believe in you, but when push comes to shove, they don't and won't fight for you. Chelsea told me from the start that despite my being funny-looking, she liked me and thought I was funny and smart. When the first executive producer of *Chelsea Lately* wanted to get rid of me, Chelsea said no. When your boss is that fiercely loyal to you, it's empowering. It also confirmed that I offer something of value to the show.

Although my trajectory was all over the board, it was really about taking advantage of every opportunity that came my way and being in the game. Comedy is my passion. Every time I think about doing something else, I realize I don't want to. Getting my master's degree in business is helping me in my career now because the business is changing and there are many new opportunities. I am able to apply some of those skills to the creative process and maximize opportunities with the digital world and other platforms. Having an MBA from USC is also a confidence booster because it gives me additional credibility with other people. I am not an expert at anything, but I do have tools that helped me shape a new way of thinking about things that have helped me grow in all aspects. I took every step to round myself out as much as I could.

Jillian Michaels

"Rejection is God's protection."

COLLEGE ATTENDED: California State University, Northridge

OCCUPATION: Personal trainer, bestselling author, and star of *The Biggest Loser*

I wanted to interview Jillian Michaels because she has always been open about feeling that learning in a traditional classroom setting wasn't for her. Despite that, she's become incredibly successful. When it comes to knowing about fitness and diet, she is one of the very best. She also is extremely comfortable with herself and owns who she is. Jillian is a kickass kind of woman.

A few years ago, Jillian came to work out with my mom and me and then proceeded to go into our pantry and refrigerator and throw away everything we had because none of it was organic or good for us. As she put it, "It's poison!" I never forgot her going through our house, and I knew I wanted her vivacious energy and story included in this book.

Going into this interview, I thought Jillian had received her college degree, but I was surprised to learn that she didn't actually graduate from college. When she told me that her reason for dropping out was that her heart wasn't in it, I understood. She is the kind of person who can't fake it if her heart isn't into something. Her story of getting to where she is today after deciding not to finish college is really amazing.

These days, it's hard to justify spending a lot of money on a college education if you aren't getting something out of it and the experience itself is making you miserable. Sometimes I think it's better to take a step back to wait and see where your life is taking you before spending a lot of time and money on something that may not pay off.

Jillian believes that everything happens for a reason and that eventually, time spent trying is never wasted. It's so important to never lose sight of who you are and be willing to expose yourself to everything you can. As Jillian puts it, "The only time you truly stall in life is when you stop trying." I thoroughly enjoyed my interview with Jillian because of her tremendous sense of humor and willingness to say what she thinks.

I was an overweight kid who carried those extra pounds into my preteens. I was bullied in junior high school and suffered a lot of humiliation over my appearance. By the time I got to tenth grade, I had gotten my nose done, had my braces removed, lost my extra weight, and transitioned from a loser to a loner. I always felt outside the social structure of high school, but never more than I did when my looks changed. I never went to parties, wasn't invited out on dates, and didn't go to my prom. By the time I got to college, I didn't understand the culture of going to fraternity parties or fit into it.

I was never really a great student. I did okay in classes that interested me, but otherwise, I had a very hard time staying focused. I have ADHD, which can be debilitating because it is difficult to slow down and focus on the things you are not interested in. I attended Cal State, Northridge, for about a year before I decided that college just wasn't for me. I wasn't passionate about being in college and my heart wasn't into it, so it didn't feel like it was where I should be. It was difficult for both of my parents when I announced that I no longer wanted to go to college. My dad is a lawyer and my mom has a Ph.D. in psychotherapy. She is an intellect who graduated magna cum laude before going on to get her master's degree. Both of my parents had spent a great deal of time pursuing higher education and weren't exactly supportive of my decision to drop out of college before I really even got started.

When I was seventeen years old, I began making older friends, most in their early twenties. That was the peer group I felt most comfortable being around, not that I was all that comfortable anywhere. I took some acting classes as a way to learn how to be relaxed around people and more outgoing. I didn't really have an interest in acting, but I just wanted to be less awkward.

At the time, I was very involved in martial arts and training for my black belt in karate. I'd gotten so good that other people thought I was a trainer. My mom helped me get my certification in high school so I could train people if I wanted to. By the time I was nineteen years old, I had gone from delivering pizzas and bartending to personal training, making two thousand dollars a week. As my personal training business grew, I began to think about opening my own gym. If I wanted to grow in the field, it seemed like the logical next step. That is, until I started dating someone who worked in Hollywood, had attended an Ivy League school, and didn't want to be dating a personal trainer who was still bartending and promoting nightclubs on the side.

I decided to fake my way into the mailroom of ICM, a Hollywood talent agency, by mocking up a college diploma that said I graduated from Cal State, Northridge. Since it was where my mom graduated from, I took her diploma, made a copy of it, matched the font on my computer, and changed the date of graduation. Once I altered the name to mine, it was complete. My plan worked, and I was hired into the agent-training program, where I spent three years working my way up through the ranks to become a motion picture packaging agent. While my job might sound like it was cool and exciting, the reality was that six months after I became an agent, I was miserable. I couldn't shake my sense that there had to be more out there than this. I was waking up feeling like I couldn't go through another day being so unhappy. There was so much stress and aggravation associated with my daily grind that it was taking a genuine toll on me. The only outlet I had was to stay on top of my health and fitness. For whatever reason, I needed to stay current on diet trends and fitness techniques.

Being an agent was hard and very unfulfilling. I'd work my ass off, and maybe, at the end of the month, I'd helped one writer get a job. Plus, I really didn't like my boss. He was trying to leave ICM and go to a competing agency, William Morris. Just before he left, I discovered that he'd done something rather unscrupulous, and I told another agent about it. Instead of firing him, they used this information as leverage to get him to stay, and let me go instead. Cutting me loose didn't hurt them. I did a great job of making that agent a powerful enemy, though.

I was twenty-seven years old and felt like I had wasted three years of my life. In a way, the time I spent at ICM was like going to college. In the end, I was no closer to figuring out what I really wanted to do with my life than I was before I started working at the agency. When you put energy into the world, it is like planting a seed. You may think you've planted an apple tree, but it doesn't bloom like you hoped. But what you might find is that three years later, you've grown an orange tree. All energy manifests. You don't always know how or when, but it will come around. It is my firm belief that in some shape or form, when you give effort to an experience, it eventually pays off. The only time you truly stall in life is when you stop trying.

I had a brief moment of fear after I was fired. I felt

lost and uncertain about the future. I didn't know what I wanted to try to do next. Fear can paralyze you, but it can also be a tremendous source of motivation when it is channeled properly. I had to make money and pay my bills, so I went back to doing what I know best, and that was training people. I was ambivalent at first, believing I had outgrown being a trainer. It was humiliating, but I had to do it. This was the only time in my life that I can truly say that I was clinically depressed. I was so out of touch with my truth and my passion. It is the worst feeling ever to lose sight of what your talent is and what your dreams are. You feel lost at sea.

I started working for a sports medicine facility, rehabbing patients under the supervision of physical therapists and chiropractors, and then graduating them into fitness training with me. The first six months were tough because my ego was a bit bruised going from Hollywood agent to physical therapy aide. They say that a bad day for your ego is a good day for your soul. I understood what that meant when a client called me to say she could feel her hip bone for the first time in eight years because she had lost so much weight working out with me.

How did I get so far away from my truth?

I had been derailed and I never saw the train coming off the track.

The universe doesn't allow you to stay out of your truth for very long. It forces you onto your path, and when it speaks, you need to listen.

I started figuring out how I was going to turn my passion for fitness into a real future. I would never allow someone else's opinion that being a trainer isn't a real job take me off course again. I took the money I had saved, along with my clients, and opened my own sports medicine facility. I have always felt that when you are in your most selfish place, that is where you are your most inspirational. Everything I have done in my work that has succeeded has been about me. My own journey to be stronger, healthier, fitter, and thinner was about me, and that led me to become an effective trainer. When you feel strong physically, you feel stronger in every facet of your life. I knew, in the same way that getting fit had transformed my self-image and self-worth, that it was a transcendent empowerment. I became passionate about my work to help other people find their strength and fitness in an authentic way. I realized that my passion wasn't just fitness, it was about sharing the very thing that saved my life.

I organically built my client list through word of mouth and by people seeing me in the gym training. By this time, I was training a lot of my former colleagues from ICM, making those three years totally worth it in the end, because one of the agents I trained put me up for *The Biggest Loser*.

I sometimes look back on my decision to drop out of college and feel insecure about my choice. These days, when I am hiring someone, I don't always look for the college degree as much as I base my decision on previous experience. My mom used to tell me that the value of college isn't just getting that ticket stamped so you can have a diploma. It helps teach you how to think. I am able to think just fine, but college does expose you to so many different things and gives you varying perspectives on the world to make you a well-rounded person. If you drop out of college, you ought to have an entrepreneurial spirit and a desire to take on the process of self-educating. I have a soft spot for people who follow their dreams despite being told otherwise. You should live your truth only. Don't live anyone else's life but your own.

Andy Cohen

"I have always felt like a success. When I got my first job, I felt like a success for getting that job, and every job I've had since. . . ."

COLLEGE ATTENDED: Boston University, bachelor's degree in broadcast journalism

OCCUPATION: Executive vice president of original programming and development, Bravo

I'm a big fan of Andy Cohen, not just of his talk show, *Watch What Happens Live*, but also because his story of finding his way to becoming a top television executive and reshaping the way we all watch TV is so cool and interesting. Andy helped create *The Real Housewives* franchise, among other huge hit shows for Bravo. Andy comes from a family who made their mark in the food business. Instead of following in their footsteps, he decided to do something crazy different to make a name for himself. He is completely self-made. He had no privileges, no doors opened for him that he didn't navigate for himself. Despite people telling him he couldn't, Andy stayed focused on his ultimate goal to someday be in front of the camera.

Whenever people ask Andy how he got to where he is in his career, he always tells them he worked his butt off. Andy's rise to becoming a top television executive was organic, but he was also aggressive in his networking. He was clear about wanting to be in New York and finding a way that led him to where he is today. He was able to gather information by blindly reaching out to people he admired and asking for their insights and suggestions along the way. He was fearless in sending handwritten notes to people he admired, which included celebrities and executives who had made it, asking them for advice and to even meet him for lunch.

There is nothing that really guides people in a step-by-step manner to figuring it all out straight from graduation. Although Andy adamantly feels there are lots of rare opportunities and jobs that didn't exist in the past for our generation, he also believes it can be overwhelming and challenging to figure out the path to get there. When Andy was starting out, he had more leeway with not knowing what he wanted to do out of college, whereas today he feels that so many of us see our indecision as a failure. I think it's really cool that someone feels that kind of empathy and compassion for the confusion of our generation because, a lot of the time, it feels like the opposite.

Andy's true appeal is that he seems like such a good person who is friendly and relatable to both his viewers and his guests. He has a tremendous understanding of pop culture and what his viewing audience wants to watch and then gives it to them. My favorite part of our interview was when I asked him if he feels like a success.

He is the only person who vehemently said, "I have always felt like a success. When I got my first job, I felt like a success for getting that job, and every job I've had since. . . ." That answer is descriptive of his personality and what he is all about . . . confidence.

<--->

I always knew I wanted to work in television, and I consider myself lucky to have that understanding. It allowed me to go out and pursue my goal. I grew up in St. Louis, in a family that is in the food business. I was the only one in our immediate family who left St. Louis with the big idea to someday make it in TV. Having that awareness early on made it easy for me to create opportunities throughout high school and college that would help inform me about the industry. Over the course of those years, I did six or seven internships with various organizations before landing a job as an intern at CBS News in New York between my junior and senior years at Boston University. Living in New York and working at a major network was incredibly cool. In fact, it was a dream come true.

After I graduated, I wanted to be in New York and work full time at CBS. I have always had a lot of confidence, and my secret desire was to be in front of the camera. While I was interning, someone at CBS told me I had a wandering eye, and because of that, I would never be considered as on-air talent. I didn't believe I had a wandering eye, but that's what they said. After my internship, I kind of gave up the dream to be on the air and focused on being the best I could be behind the scenes. I would rather move to New York and not be in front of the camera than not be involved in television at all. Still, deep down, I really wanted to be on camera. My big plan was to move from small market to small market, which is typically what on-air talent does to hone their skills.

I made a lot of contacts when I worked as an intern and thought I could wait tables until I found the right job at the network. When I was an intern at CBS, I had one newswriting and reporting assignment to interview someone famous whom I admired and do a profile on them. I wrote letters to Susan Lucci's and Sam Donaldson's publicists. To my surprise, Susan actually agreed to go to lunch with me so I could interview her!

Networking and anything you do that is deliberate has to be organic. To me, it's about being passionate and letting that enthusiasm show. I always let my passion guide me to be better at my job, and because of that, it helped me build my career. I'd spent six months working as a waiter when I heard that someone I knew at CBS was being promoted, so there was an opening for an assistant job in the news division. I got very lucky and was excited to be offered any entry-level position. I wasn't nervous because I had already spent time working in the same department when I was an intern, and because of that I felt ready for it. I was happy being an assistant, and I was a good assistant too. I showed up with my enthusiastic manner to the job every day, and people took notice. It didn't take me long to get my first promotion.

I spent ten years working at CBS, eventually serving as the senior producer for *The Early Show*. I was also a producer for *48 Hours* and *CBS This Morning*. I spent my time learning the ins and outs of producing news segments and stories, interviewing people from all walks of life, and sharpening my skills. From the moment I got my first job at CBS, I have felt like a success. I was in the door, and that was all I needed. Every job going forward took me to the next level of success.

In July 2000, I decided to move to a cable channel called Trio, where I was named vice president of original programming. My job was to create new, fresh programming for the network and to oversee existing shows that were already on the air. Four years into that position, NBC/Universal took over Trio, and I wasn't sure what I would do next.

At the time, Logo was launching as the first advertiser-supported commercial television channel in the United States geared toward the LGBT community. It was founded by a former MTV executive, so there was no doubt that it would be cutting edge and an exciting place to work. I wanted to be the head of programming. When I interviewed with Logo, I didn't get the job. I couldn't get over that they didn't hire me. I was disappointed and thought they were crazy for not giving me the position.

Bravo was courting me too, but initially, I was indifferent to the opportunity. After Logo passed me over, I reluctantly took a position with Bravo as senior vice president of original programming and development because I wanted to keep working in television. I'd spent fourteen years developing as a producer and becoming a respected executive. Although I hadn't shared it with a lot of people, I still had a strong desire to be in front of the camera. I started a blog on BravoTV.com, and at the time I was the only executive at the network to have one. Because of that, I started being interviewed about TV programming. My boss wanted to do an online companion show to *Top Chef* and, out of the blue, suggested I host it and make it an extension of my blog. This unexpected opportunity organically transitioned me from executive to on-air host. I was thrilled, especially when the network asked me to host the first *Real Housewives of Orange County* reunion show. I had helped create the *Real Housewives* brand for the network, so I knew the cast and show inside and out. It was a perfect match. As my presence on Bravo grew, so did the executives' interest in having me take the show I was doing online and turn it into a weekly show we could put on the air once a week at midnight. That was the genesis of *Watch What Happens Live*, which now airs five days a week. I was in my glory, doing what I loved most: working in television, creating programming, and doing my thing on the air five days a week.

I am glad I am not starting out today. Not only do you have so many companies downsizing, which makes it harder to get a job, you are coming out of one of the worst recessions in the country's history. On the other hand, there are so many more possibilities in media than there were when I was coming up the ranks. There are more shows, more channels, more production companies, and more vehicles of distribution. The pressure you put on yourself is crazy. The representation of twenty-year-olds in the media is that you sit around watching *Gossip Girl* where everyone has a great wardrobe, is overachieving, and has lots of money. Obviously, the real world isn't like that, but the sense that it should be is ever-present for your generation, which is terribly unfair.

When I graduated, I feel like society allowed me to have more allowances to figure things out. From what I can tell, all you hear today is, "Why haven't you figured it out yet?" If I were going to hire you, I want someone who is good at their job. I don't care how many followers you have on Twitter. In fact, I want you to be all about supporting me and not blabbing on Twitter and Facebook about what a hard day you had at work. To me, less is more. I want to hire people who I can tell really want to work. They're qualified, and their résumés show that they have gone out of their way to work in TV. They all had internships and have spent time working as an assistant or doing the small jobs. That shows me dedication, commitment, and desire to be in the business.

If you are interviewing for a job, any job, the worst thing you can do is say, "I am checking this out to see if it is something I am interested in." To me, if you're just "checking things out," don't do it on my time or my dime. It costs employers money to bring someone on and train them. For six months, you are a cost, not an asset. I can't take the risk of hiring you to discover that the job wasn't right for you. Be committed to doing what you love and being the best at whatever it is you're doing.

Nicole Williams

*"Excellence is like a muscle. If you apply it,
no matter what job you're doing, people notice."*

COLLEGE ATTENDED: University of British Columbia
OCCUPATION: LinkedIn career expert, author, and entrepreneur

Nicole Williams is one of the most positive and up-
beat people I've met. She's feisty, forward, and full of
great information. Nicole is a real cheerleader for other
women, which is so refreshing to see. Although I didn't
know her before this interview, she seems like one of
those girlfriends you long to have—the ones who don't
get jealous or feel threatened by someone else's success
and always want the best for you. As a young woman
going into the work world, that's an inspiring quality
to have.

Nicole has a great story. Although she grew up in
a trailer park and was told she'd never amount to anything, she still went out into the world and created her
own destiny by building a career counseling consulting
company. Nicole seemed to be confident and motivated
at a very early age. I think she focused on things that

would motivate her, especially proving people wrong in getting out of the trailer park and following her dreams no matter how ridiculous others thought they were.

Nicole spoke candidly about the differences between men and women in the workplace, even comparing it to dating, and offered some amazing advice on how to manage emotional stress at the workplace. I found it interesting to hear her thoughts on how men attack their careers head-on while women overthink it and are more emotional and introverted. The most important thing to remember is to be confident, secure, and ready to roll up your sleeves and work.

When I was a little girl, my mom worked in a paint factory. She was a single mom who worked in an environment that sucked the life out of her. Watching that day in and day out as a kid, and seeing how it affected her, scared me. I swore I'd never live that life. Seeing my mom so unhappy in her career shaped my idea about what work should be when I grew up—which was on the complete opposite side of the spectrum of how my mom lived. Ultimately, we all want to do what we love and what we are passionate about.

Early on, I became curious about what other people did for their career. I was always full of questions.

"How do you get into that?"

"What did you study?"

"What kind of skills do you need?"

"How much money do you make?"

I was an investigative young woman who was trying to figure it all out. I've always been infatuated with discovering career skills, building relationships, asking great questions, and learning how to position myself for success.

After I graduated, I knew I wanted to work in the world of careers. I started at the Canadian National Institute for the Blind as their director of career and technology. I was working in a restaurant, paying my way through school, when I was offered the job. This was my first awakening that there is opportunity all around. If you are a person who acts with integrity and tries your hardest at your job, regardless of where you're working, people notice. Being prepared and doing your best means that, at some point, you will encounter opportunity.

I took the job at CNIB as a way of building my career and resources. Two years in, the nonprofit organization was audited by an outside consulting firm. A woman from the consulting firm took me under her wing and soon offered me a job. At the time, I was studying for my MBA at Cambridge. I wasn't sure I wanted to quit graduate school.

"Come work for me and I will give you an MBA's worth of experience. Forget the degree!" she insisted.

How could I say no?

The company's clients included the UN and the World Trade Organization (WTO), as well as other great companies and organizations. I started working as a consultant doing a number of projects. It was there that I started to look for career advice and couldn't find it. That was when I decided that I would build a company that would help young women create success. I had no clue what I wanted to do when I was starting out other than wanting to work in and around career counseling. And there was nobody to help me. If I was feeling this way, I presumed other women would feel some essence of how I felt and would be less alone in their career pursuit.

I grew up in a trailer park. When I told people I wanted to write a book, everyone told me there was no way I would ever do it.

A lot of people want to fall back on some reason they "can't" get a job, buy a car, buy a home, figure out what they want to do, find a boyfriend, whatever. I always tell my clients to get past the excuses, news, unemployment rate, and statistics. In other words, everyone and everything that is telling you that it is impossible. My advice is to turn off the news! I know it sounds crazy, but there is so much crap out there that is meant to scare people or generate viewers. The bad news stops people before they even get started. If you buy into those reasons, it will become your reality. Why would you look for a job when unemployment is teetering just below 10 percent, and you probably won't get hired anyway? So many people quit before they even get started because of their attachment to the news, which is focused more on fear than truth. Don't be one of those people biding their time waiting for the economy to get better. Be the person who says, "Screw this, I am not going to sit back and wait anymore. I am going out to do this!" This attitude makes you one of the few instead of one of many. There are plenty of opportunities out there, especially for the person who is willing to take a risk and try the thing that feels beyond them. Writing a book felt like it was something so much bigger than me. It was my calling and something I needed to do. You create greatness in life by virtue of persevering and working hard and being disciplined. The better you understand why you are doing something, the more likely you are to get through the hard times that usually make people give up and quit.

Men tend to dive into their career and learn as they go. They get better and better by virtue of experience. On the other hand, women want to feel that we are perfectly prepared. We get this from school. I have a friend who is an acclaimed director, but when she was first starting her career right out of school, she wanted to keep taking more courses because she didn't feel quite ready yet. She wasn't "prepared" for the real world. I remember her telling me she read George Lucas's story to be inspired and passively attempting to get information. Reading books wasn't getting her behind a camera making movies. We learn the most and excel the fastest when we are engaged and doing things—even trying and failing.

Another common mistake women make in the workplace is taking things too personally. I have run a test on a group of students that always makes this point. I will get a guy from the group to come up and ask me for a job or a raise and I will say, "no." Then I ask a woman to do the same and give the same answer.

When I ask each participant how my response made them feel, men externalize it. They say, "I think you're a bitch." "I think the economy sucks." "I think you don't have the budget to hire me." "I think you don't have room in the company."

Conversely, women internalize their answers by saying, "I didn't ask correctly." "I asked too loud." "I asked too soft." "Maybe I didn't deserve it." "I'm not ready yet." They feel too personally attached to the outcome.

If you're a woman in the workplace, I think there is a great need to separate your personal self from your professional self. It will allow you to be stronger, strive harder, and take bigger risks. A lot of women make the mistake of thinking they want to straddle the career thing for a while because they ultimately want to get married and have kids. For most, that decision can be as far as ten years away, and they're already using it to half-ass their performance. Men never think that. They go in and put everything they've got into their career. They don't expect that they are going to have to stop and balance their life. Men just go. At the end of the day, your career is dependent on you: your sense of self, confidence, and motivation. These are the core factors that lead to success.

When I was in my thirties, I was coming off a devastating divorce. Even though it was my decision, this was a very hard time in my life. My girlfriends decided to do something to cheer me up and get me back out there to start dating. They gave me a basket filled with all sorts of goodies, including lingerie and a copy of the book *The Rules*. One night, I was skimming the pages of the book as a way to reconnect myself to the concepts of dating. As I read, I began thinking, *This is great career advice. What if I took those basic tactics used to land a man and applied them to cultivating a career?* They were simple and universal.

- *Keep it brief*
- *Don't bash your ex*
- *Have others sing your praises*
- *Play hard to get*
- *Keep the fire alive*
- *Be willing to walk away*
- *Don't give the milk away for free*

The translation of dating advice into career advice made a lot of sense. You wouldn't go on a first date and start bashing your exes any more than you would go on an interview and talk about your former bosses. Playing hard to get and being discerning works for your dating life as well as in your professional life. Technology has changed the game a bit. How you position yourself technologically will determine whom you are going to attract. There is a hard balance between revealing your true self and your best self. Your employer doesn't want to know more than your date does, especially in the "getting to know you" stage. What attracts employers and dates is a feeling of mystery and that you are in demand. Have standards, but allow yourself the opportunity to explore as much as you can and just go for it.

For those of you coming out of college who have little or no work experience, one of the best things you can do to help boost your opportunities is to reveal who you are and become discoverable while being strategic about the image you are putting out there. LinkedIn is a great place to start because you can follow the companies that you are interested in working for. If you do that, you learn about upcoming product releases and who is coming and going within the company. When you are in college or graduating, you can search your alumni. When I did this for the first time, I searched the school I graduated from, the University of British Columbia. Next, I searched those results to see how many people worked in media. Then I found out how many of those people lived in New York City. I was able to come up with a handful that shared all of these things in common with me and reached out to initiate building valuable professional relationships.

It's important to remember that being searchable works both ways. These days, lots of employers search the 200-million-plus members on LinkedIn based on skill set, experience, school affiliations, connections, and relationships. If you are not searchable by these traits and factors, no one can find you. The majority of people on LinkedIn aren't being searched by their name, so it's important to fill out your LinkedIn profile and join the industry groups within the site to listen to the conversations that industry gurus are having. Thousands of professional groups are easily accessible, and many answer questions about career advice and opportunities. Their responses are attached to their professional association, so you won't get a string of responses like you would on a regular message board.

Here are some great tips to getting noticed:

1. *Check your spelling.*
2. *Don't assume people know you.*
3. *Just because you are behind a computer doesn't mean you can be rude or inappropriate any more than you would be in person.*
4. *Don't go dark. If you are communicating with someone, keep the conversation going until it is done.*
5. *Don't burn bridges. A year from now you may need that person you just blew off, were rude to, or didn't get back to.*

Sometimes college students don't ask for that big connection request because they think the person will deny them. Often it is the most senior people within an organization who aren't being approached for a mentorship or being asked how they got into the industry they lead. These are all questions those people love to answer about themselves. Don't be shy. Reach out and build those relationships. Today's technology makes it easier to connect. You are not writing a letter and mailing it to London—you can send a connection request on LinkedIn or via e-mail. All it takes is initiative and courage to make an impact.

Armin van Buuren

"It goes beyond liking, and beyond a hobby; it's about a way of living. Music is essential to my life."

COLLEGE ATTENDED: Stedelijk Gymnasium Leiden; Leiden University, degree in law

OCCUPATION: Trance music producer and DJ

When thinking about different career paths of people for this book, I decided I wanted to interview a well-known DJ because I think their trajectories are often similar to those of others who try to turn their passion into a career. It's not as easy as it looks.

My initial thought about interviewing a DJ was to talk about how someone turns their love of music into a high-paying career. I think most people my age believe that becoming a DJ is an easy transition from college or any stage in life, especially if they've been in a party phase and are going into the real world. I was surprised to discover that it's not only a difficult career path but also a field where most people never make it. Armin is one of a handful of DJs who have successfully made it to the very top. Only ten people in the world do what Armin does at the level he has achieved, and getting to where he is wasn't easy. He spent fifteen years becoming the world's most popular DJ, carving out a niche in a very small market.

Armin is extremely well educated and highly strategic about his career and life. He understands the business side of music every bit as much as he does the creative side. When I asked why he wanted to become a DJ, he explained that although being a DJ is great and a lot of people want to do what he does, it is also incredibly challenging. You need to know what you are doing because it isn't as easy as it seems. It is a discouraging business, one where things don't always go your way. It's a lot like acting in that way. It takes a long time to break into the industry and reach the point where you are actually making a living at it and can rely on it as a source of income.

Armin is a man driven by an unbridled and relentless passion for music. As a self-described perfectionist, he is always striving to stay on top of the music scene he's helped to grow. Armin is known as one of the great innovators of the trance movement and has since gone on to found Armada Music, his own record label, which has been named Best Global Record label four years in a row and has twenty-five sublabels under its banner. One of the greatest pieces of wisdom Armin focused on was the importance of having something to fall back on in case music didn't work out for him. This is especially true if you are going to go after a career that has a low rate of success. I was surprised to learn that Armin chose to get a law degree as his backup plan to doing music. Even after his career began to take off, he continued his study of law, eventually earning his master's degree in 2002. While he hasn't had a need to practice law, it definitely comes in handy as a great resource and tool he can rely on during business deals and negotiations. I think it's brilliant to combine two opposite professions and have them work hand in hand throughout your career.

I was born into a musical family where I was allowed to indulge my passion for music from a young age. I spent all the money I earned from my paper route as a young boy on records. My mom won a computer when I was ten years old, which immediately got my interest. I was a little nerdy kid writing my own BASIC programs, learning about technology as I experimented along the way. I had an immediate love of music, especially dance music. It had this great rebellious sound that was so different from the "beautiful" songs I heard on the radio. I started making low-profile mix tapes for friends, and as I got more experienced, I began making higher-profile mixes. I was heavily influenced by electronica pioneer Jean Michel Jarre as well as Dutch producer Ben Liebrand, who ironically ended up mentoring me years later on my mixing and producing skills.

I went to college with the idea that I wanted to become a doctor. In Holland, the medical school system is set up like a lottery that allows only a few students a year to enroll in medical school, so I ended up studying law instead. I made a deal with my father that I could continue to pursue my interest in electronic music as long as I finished my law degree.

Electronica was a passion, but it started out as a hobby. I didn't want to have the pressure of needing a big hit or a high-paying gig to cover my rent and other living expenses. Music was a hobby I could do on the side, but I never saw it becoming my main way of making a living. While I was attending law school, I was doing some DJ'ing in the U.K. and I had some chart success in 1999 and early 2000 with an instrumental dance track called "Communication." After that song hit, people started booking me as a DJ. At the time, I was working as a clerk in a law firm too. It wasn't a conscious decision to pursue music over law. It was more of a pause until I could figure out where music was taking me.

In June 2001, I launched the first episode of my own radio show called *A State of Trance*. Twelve years later, I still host the weekly two-hour show, where I present the biggest EDM tunes of the moment and provide an interactive way for fans to discover new music. My radio show had a lot to do with catapulting my career to the next level because it gave me an outlet to make myself known to fans of my style of music and put me in the position to build my brand through becoming a trend spotter.

Even though I was making a little bit of money working as a DJ and from my radio show, I finished law school and got my degree in 2002. I spent six months juggling my career in music and working at a law firm. It was a tough combination because my work as a DJ had me in clubs on the weekends, staying up late at night, and my job at the law firm required me to be in the office early in the morning during the weekdays. It was clear to me that music was my passion.

At the time, I had no mortgage or family to support. I was free and clear of any real financial obligations because I was still living at my parents' house. I built a studio there, so when I wasn't on the road, I was home creating music. While my parents were supportive of my career, they weren't crazy about the constant boom, boom, boom sounds they heard coming from the studio. They never stopped me, though. Besides, I had fulfilled the deal I'd made with my dad to get my law degree, so I could do whatever I wanted.

EDM really began to take off in 2002, the same year I graduated from law school. I had a steady stream of playing smaller gigs, but as the radio show grew, so did my audience, and larger venues began to come into play.

Although being a lawyer was never my ambition, I have zero regret about taking the time to go to law school. I remember being in class one morning when my professor walked into the room and drew a tree of all of the companies he had shares of stock in. At the time, I thought it was boring. A few years later, I had a tree just like that for myself. Most of what I studied in law school was boring to me because the first few years were mostly spent getting a basic knowledge about the law and how the system works. When I zeroed in on the area of business law, it became interesting. Law school taught me the fundamentals of doing research, which I enjoyed and surprisingly has come in handy in my career as a business owner today. Having a working knowledge of the law, especially tax and copyright law, has helped me stay current on issues that affect my businesses and me. I can read contracts and understand what they mean without having to rely on other people for guidance. It also gave me direction when it came to making career decisions that would help propel my success forward.

Studying made me very disciplined and helped me understand the true meaning of being focused. Getting a college degree requires a great deal of self-control that shouldn't be discounted. Every day you get up, have breakfast, start your schoolwork, and focus on your studies. Being in the music business requires the same kind of discipline. I have always pushed myself hard, taking on more than my fair share of responsibility and always doing the work it takes to succeed. Without going to school and getting my master's in law, I am not sure I would be as successful as I am today. Setting up a company, being focused, and making concrete plans instead of waiting around for something to happen requires taking action. You need discipline if you want something in life, and then you need a plan to get it.

When deciding what you want to do in life, my advice is to pick a trade that gives you some stability. Choose a career that is solid and have something to fall back on. If you do that, you will always have a resource to turn to for money. I know the world of DJ'ing seems like a mecca for a lot of people and is an inspiration for them, especially the idea of traveling around the world, playing big gigs, and being paid a lot of money. There are only ten or fifteen DJs around the world who can do what I do. I am very aware that I got lucky. Don't quit your studies with the ambition of becoming a DJ. It's a big gamble. There are no guarantees in life, especially when it comes to electronic music.

If you decide to go for something in life, whatever it is, make your own name doing it. Think about what you can bring to the table that makes you different from the others in your chosen field. Identify why other people would want to pay money to see you. Don't try to be the next Armin van Buuren, because there is already an Armin van Buuren. Why copy someone else? An audience can go out and see the real thing. Find what makes you unique. You can't try a little bit and expect a huge result. Commit 100 percent of yourself to achieving your dream. You will have good days and bad days, but there is always something to learn from the experiences you have along the way.

In Holland, we have a saying: "You need to learn how to divide before you can multiply." I was lucky to surround myself with good mentors and advisors early in my career. It was hard for me to put my trust and my career in the hands of other people. But I learned so much from each and every one of them, whether it was about the pitfalls and dangers of dealing with crooked people who work in the music business or guidance building up Armada Music.

I was always advised by the right people. You need to have a gut feeling about whom you choose to work with and if they are the right kind of associates to help you in your career. It wasn't easy for me to learn to trust my gut, and there were times I questioned decisions, but when you surround yourself with the right people, the ones who truly have your back, you are free to ask and they will not hesitate to give you an answer. You may not like what you hear, but the truth is always better than smoke and mirrors.

Meghan McCain

*"I consider myself mildly successful
because I have been able to continue doing
the things I love. . . ."*

COLLEGE ATTENDED: Columbia University, bachelor's degree in art history

OCCUPATION: Author, columnist, talk show host

I met Meghan McCain for the first time when she spoke at the Women's Conference my mother hosted in 2010 when she was First Lady of California. Not long after that introduction, I interviewed Meghan a couple of times while I was doing some work for an entertainment news show and we've since been able to work together on various projects. As I got to know Meghan, I realized that we have a lot in common, and we are both women who aren't afraid to say what's on our minds. Though I am a little shyer than she is, I think Meghan is incredibly gutsy for never backing down from saying exactly how she feels, what she thinks, and where she stands. She doesn't put a censor on her thoughts just to appease others. She is so real and brutally honest, traits that I greatly admire.

Every time I ran into Meghan, she was always so kind and supportive of me and the things I was doing. I can relate to her on so many levels, especially her strength to face down those who judge, hate, or place their values on others. I also respect her for holding her head up, finding her independence, and creating her own path. Staying true to who you are is sometimes hard when other people place judgments on you, but it's important to never lose sight of what you value and what you believe in and to find the courage to take on whatever challenges you may face in pursuit of your dreams. Meghan is a great example of someone who lives her life that way and continues to march to her own beat.

←———————————————————————————→

There are a lot of misconceptions about leaving college and heading into the real world, but one of the biggest is that it is going to be easy. The idea that there is something great waiting for you on the other side of graduation is sadly naïve. I decided to major in art history because I had put off my choice until I was forced to. I liked art history and had taken enough classes to get me close to graduation. If I had changed majors that late, I would have put myself behind because I would have needed to take too many other classes to graduate. I never saw myself as a curator or a gallery owner—and I never saw myself going for my master's because I didn't have the desire to be a true art historian either. I wasn't really sure what I wanted to do, but I wasn't going to let that stop me from finishing college and moving on with my life.

I envy people who know what they want to do right out of college—those who can follow a straightforward path toward becoming a doctor, lawyer, or CPA. In many ways, that kind of direct approach seems so much easier than having to figure it all out. I didn't have a clue about what I really wanted to do, so I did what a lot of other kids do—I went home to live with my parents in Phoenix until I could figure it out.

About a month and a half after I graduated in 2007, my father announced his candidacy for president. Instead of focusing on what I wanted to do with the rest of my life, I decided to make up every excuse I could think of to avoid finding a job so I could go to work on his campaign. I didn't want to sit around aimlessly doing nothing, and I really didn't want to get a job simply for the paycheck—so I begged my dad to let me go on the road with him. I can admit that I was curious about what it would be like to see his campaign from the inside and I really wanted to support him in any way I could. Much to my surprise, however, my father didn't want me to work for the campaign because he was well aware that politics weren't my main interest, and therefore, I wouldn't be a good fit.

While attending Columbia, I had the opportunity to intern at *Newsweek*. I did a lot to help develop their website and had great success in writing pop culture pieces in a political environment, so I had some experience blogging going into the campaign. I knew I had the ability to hit the road and make a positive contribution to my father's campaign. All I had to do was convince him and his team. I came up with the idea to write about my experiences. I called my blog the McCain Blogette, where I mused about life on the campaign trail as well as my interest in fashion, music, and pop culture. At first, my dad's political advisors didn't like the idea of me writing about the campaign, but by that time, I had built up enough of a following to create something that could potentially have a positive impact. To reach my widest audience, I decided to launch a campaign website, which not only gave me the platform to post my blogs, it also gave me a purpose—so they let me do it. At the time, it was something new, hip, and extremely different for the Republican Party and was designed to bring in a younger demographic. I was grateful to have the opportunity and even more appreciative to have a job.

After the campaign ended, I was faced with the reality that I still didn't know what I wanted to do. I went into a post–campaign/graduation depression where I was the most miserable I'd ever been in my life. It's easy to feel depressed when you're not working or accomplishing something more with your life, because the expectation when you graduate is that you should be taking the world by storm. I had spent several months on the road with my dad, feeling like I was accomplishing something, and then suddenly I found myself back home again, with nothing to do and no plan to figure out my next steps. I don't think what I was feeling was so unusual, it was just delayed. I was sad, began to gain a lot of weight, and didn't know what I wanted to do next.

Though I didn't realize it at the time, looking back, I regret my decision to move back home after the campaign. For a lot of people, I think that decision is necessary because of finances, but for others, it can also become a crutch. I have friends who moved back into their parents' homes and never left. And why would they when their mom is cooking their meals, their laundry is getting done, and there is no cost of living? It's very easy and appealing, but it isn't helping prepare you to become an independent adult. Moving back in with your parents arrests your development. For me, it was the wrong decision.

I didn't wallow for very long because it was pretty clear that I needed help to figure things out and move on with my life. I began talking to friends and family and e-mailing acquaintances I'd made on the road asking their advice on what I should do next. I asked a few people if they had any interest in having me write blogs for them because that was the only thing I had done since graduating and felt like I was good at, and I really liked writing them. In the meantime, I began to set up meetings and a few job interviews. Some of the places I went to didn't feel right or felt like an environment where I wouldn't fit in. It took a few months until I finally found the job I had been waiting for—and it was a perfect fit. In 2009, my search led me to a new website called *The Daily Beast*. This position became my home base for the next four and a half years. Being a part of this successful startup was a great experience that helped launch my writing career.

Jared Eng

*"You are in the wrong room if you
are the smartest person in the room."*

COLLEGE ATTENDED: Columbia University, bachelor's degree in computer science

OCCUPATION: Founder and editor in chief, JustJared.com and JustJaredJr.com

In a world full of tabloid media and a constant bombardment of negative photos of celebrities, I love that there is a place where people can go to get their "celebrity gossip" without the hurt. Jared Eng, founder of JustJared.com, has made his mark as a celebrity blogger by being nice about celebrities. It's one of the reasons I enjoy visiting his site. It features pictures of celebrities going about their day, doing regular things. He posts celebrity gossip without all of the terrible comments other sites feature, which I find refreshing in the media today.

Jared realized that he had an obsession for celebrity life when he first became exposed to it in college. Jared grew up extremely sheltered, raised by parents who believed that studying was far more important than watching TV. When he realized he had a passion for pop culture, he decided to channel his obsession with celebrity by creating something that didn't exist—a *positive* celebrity blog.

Although he didn't set out to become a professional blogger, his website ended up taking off. Today, JustJared.com has grown into a full-fledged brand, even establishing partnership deals with Lacoste and other brands. Jared maintains his own studio to record video interviews with celebrities and directs a staff of five people, including his older brother, making JustJared .com a family business his parents can be proud of.

I studied computer science in college because my parents thought that was a safe choice that would guarantee me a job after I graduated. I didn't really like it, but I stuck with it to make my parents happy. College wasn't all that interesting to me because it focused more on theoretical stuff instead of real-world applications. To make up for my lack of interest in school, I did a lot of internships throughout college, including MTV and an artist's studio. I also traveled as much as I could, whether it was with my church or just to change up the scenery from living in New York. While the social experience of going to college was good, I wish it had been more worth my time.

I grew up in a pretty sheltered home where I was

allowed to watch only thirty minutes of TV a week. My parents stressed academia, so I was pretty much a geek. I didn't know a lot about pop culture until I got to college and started writing about the songs I was listening to and the television and movies I was watching. I loved writing about this stuff so much it became a passion of mine. The more I wrote, the more people were reading. I was trying to be a little more sassy and opinionated than I am, which took a lot of effort because it wasn't authentic. I worked hard to come up with splashy headlines that were creative and witty. Being crafty was fun, but it wasn't really who I am.

When I graduated, it turned out that my degree wasn't as applicable as I expected it to be. I didn't really know what I wanted to do either, which was a bigger problem. Looking back, I wish I had taken more initiative to talk to people and network a bit more to see what jobs interested me instead of focusing on a career based on my major.

I finally took a job at Time, Inc. analyzing magazine distribution. I didn't need any special qualifications—just a willingness to be a hard worker, reliable, and fast on the computer. Since I can type quickly, this seemed like a good place to start. When I wasn't working, I spent most of my free time blogging about celebrities and pop culture. In 2005, the blog was doing well enough, making almost all of our revenue from the sale of display ads, that I thought I could start a business blogging. Growing up, I always had a personal blog, which was more like a journal that I kept to myself, but I didn't know that blogging could be an

actual profession. I never aspired to be a blogger or journalist; it just happened. I changed the tone of my blog to a
kinder, gentler version than I had been writing in college
and began to cover more of my interests instead of letting
my readers decide on the content. I wanted to put the kind
of product out into the world I'd want to receive. I respect
people, and they respect me. Being nice in my blogs came
more naturally. I was finding my own path and a way out
of corporate America when I decided to go pro. When I
felt like it was a secure decision, I quit my job and turned
JustJared.com into a full-time career.

My parents weren't completely sure I was making the
right decision. They had sent me to Columbia to study
computer science because they wanted me to pursue a
professional path. They couldn't understand that blogging
could be a real profession. Even when I started making
money blogging, my parents still thought I should pursue
something more traditional.

When the blog started growing, it became a little bit of
an obsession. Despite the obvious perks of the job, it is far
from glamorous. I post about sixty-five items per day, seven
days a week, from the moment I wake up—sometimes at
five a.m.—to the time I go to sleep. Sometimes I don't
sleep at all.

When I started blogging, I didn't know a single person
in Hollywood. I wasn't familiar with any of the other pop
culture bloggers either. I am not a really outgoing guy who
will approach other people to network or meet. It took a
lot of effort for me to blindly e-mail people out of the blue

JARED ENG

and make contact over Facebook, Twitter, and Instagram. Slowly, I started going to events as much as possible, which made it easier to meet people, get their cards and contact information, and then follow up. As a result, I have a huge Rolodex of contacts. It became a domino effect that grew into a wide variety of social circles. Even though it was initially out of my comfort zone, I put myself on the front lines to meet people and shared who I am as a person and where I wanted to go. If you don't put yourself out there, people can't and won't help you.

Laysha Ward

"Leave things better than you found them."

COLLEGE ATTENDED: Indiana University, bachelor's degree in journalism; University of Chicago, master's degree in social services administration

OCCUPATION: Target Corporation, President of Community Relations and the Target Foundation

Target is one of those companies that completely understands their customer—someone trying to live life, staying hip to trends and necessities, without breaking the bank. A day rarely goes by when I don't see a Target ad on TV, in a magazine, or on a billboard. Laysha Ward is the woman, brains, and genius behind their brilliant marketing strategies.

I first met Laysha when she agreed to have Target as one of the main sponsors for the California Governor's Conference for Women. She would kick off every conference with a speech about why she personally loved the empowerment of women, and why Target wanted to be a part of spreading the word, or as the Women's Conference states it, "passing it on." I have always been a huge fan of Target and all of the campaigns they choose to involve themselves in because they are always right on point with their message and find a way to make the brand accessible for everyone.

Laysha always knew that in order to get her foot in the door for any opportunities that should come her way, she needed to get a good education. Knowing that her biggest passion was giving back, she decided to apply for jobs that helped her stay true to who she is.

Being aware of your finances and understanding the meaning of being smart with your money is a huge part of the transition out of college. Laysha grew up being financially aware, but she had to be extra cautious when balancing the growth of her career while taking out loans for her master's program.

Lucky for us, Laysha and her team at Target totally get what it's like coming out of college today. They have campaigns that promote the importance of getting a good education and raise money to keep kids in school. Whether it is promoting education or being aware of saving money, Laysha doesn't just talk the talk, she walks the walk on a level that most of us can only imagine.

$\longleftrightarrow$

My great-grandmother taught me that there are a few things in life worth fighting for: faith, family, freedom, and education. She was 105 years old when she passed away in 1985. She was born twenty years after the end of slavery and made it clear to me that education was an important ticket out of poverty and into opportunity—opportunity she never saw in her lifetime.

I am the first person in my family who got into college and graduated. While college is one component of preparation, it is not the only component. It was a single step in the journey. Going to college gives you a leg up, and having some form of secondary education is a pathway out of poverty and provides many opportunities. Having a quality education, regardless of race or socioeconomic level, is part of achieving the American dream and a big contributing factor that helped me achieve that dream.

I changed my major more than a few times while attending Indiana University. Eventually, I found myself a fifth-year senior and still not quite sure of what I wanted to do. Service work was in my DNA, so I hoped to find something that would allow me to follow that desire. My passion for giving back started with my family. We are influenced by many forces in our lives, and often those forces are our first teachers, who are usually our parents or caring adults who helped us grow up. When I was a child, my influencers were my parents, my teachers, and my church, where I learned that service is the price you pay for living on the planet. Even though we came from limited means, we never used that as an excuse for not being a part of the solution.

While I was thinking about possible jobs, I applied to the Peace Corps. I was living in Chicago, waiting on an assignment, when I took a job in sales at a department store called Marshall Field's. The job paid an hourly wage and required me to work all of the varying shifts you would expect for an entry-level retail position. I learned about the retail business at a grassroots level and am forever grateful for the experience. I didn't know anyone who had worked in a corporation before, so it wasn't in my worldview or my experience. Much to my surprise, the company was committed to giving back 5 percent of its profits to the community and promoting volunteering and public service. That type of giving from a company was a foreign concept to me. I didn't even know jobs or companies like that existed. I was blown away. This knowledge was a pivotal moment in my life because I realized that I could learn about business and also do things that were good for the community.

I got involved in the community giving activities and observed how the company allocated grants and was involved in service. This deep exposure to charity practices provided me with a firm understanding of how the entire organization worked. This knowledge was a great asset when I moved into a management position.

When I was deciding whether to go to graduate school, it became apparent that in the future, a master's degree would be just as important as my B.A. At some point, in order to make the leap to the next level in my career, I would need to have an incremental credential. I felt that as a woman and as a woman of color, it would make a big difference in my career growth and would be an important point of differentiation.

I had a lot to consider in deciding to go to grad

school, especially analyzing the cost in attaining that degree. Managing your finances and money is one of the most essential things you will do in your life. You have to be smart about what that means. I had someone teach me early on that when you create a budget, it should include your lifelong learning as a part of that plan. When you are applying and looking at schools, you have to assess what all of the costs are going to be. For me, I needed to decide if I wanted to stay in Illinois or go out of state. Would I go to a private university or a public state school? Where would I live? What were the class expenses and the cost of books and lab fees? Would I commute, and would I need to buy a car? I needed to think holistically about those expenses and how I would pay for them. It was important to be careful because I had student loans that I was already paying from going to Indiana University. If I took out a student loan for grad school, I needed to look at the total payment and the required timeline to pay both loans back. I didn't want to spend the next sixty years of my life paying off big student loans.

Being raised in a family with limited means, I was constantly aware of our financial resources. Part of my upbringing was always making sure we had enough money to cover the week's bills. I grew up with a sensitivity to finances and in a household where going to college wasn't a given. My older sister didn't immediately go to college. She enlisted in the military instead to save money and to have access to resources to pay for college after she served our country. I was brought up in an environment where there was always the thought, "How are we going to find the resources and how will I pay this off?" I understood from an early age that there is no "free lunch." If I was going to graduate school, I would have to give up some freedom, whether by not hanging out with my friends as much or getting a second job to help pay the expenses. When I weighed everything out, it was worth all of the sacrifice.

I was fortunate to have good mentors in my life who had been down the path before me and who were more sophisticated and experienced. They shared their words of wisdom and gave advice that helped me make the right decisions along the way. A few made it clear that choosing not to go to graduate school wasn't an option for me. These were people that I trusted, who said I could do it now or later, but either way, I had to get my master's degree. They advised me to think about where I wanted to go and what I wanted to study. They also advised me to study something I was passionate about, rather than what other people thought was best for me, because I would be paying for that education. I would also be spending a long time doing the work and applying the information gained from the experience. I asked myself, "What do I want to learn in graduate school? Do I want to continue to make a contribution and be a lifelong learner?" If so, no one else's opinion mattered more than my own. I needed to pause and reflect on what was most important and how I could take my talents and leverage them best. It was helpful to have a coach to talk through my decision with, especially when it came to considering everything from the cost to the minutiae. It all was factored into my final assessment.

I decided to enroll in the master's program at the University of Chicago. I worked full time during the day and went to graduate school part time in the evenings. Going back to school was a sacrifice of time because it became a second full-time job. I had commitments during the day that couldn't suffer as a result of my pursuit of a higher education. I was in a relationship that needed attention too. My boyfriend has his Ph.D., and it helped to have a partner who understood the financial and time constraints of graduate school. Luckily, he also appreciated the rewards. Still, it was challenging. Since I was attending school part time, getting my degree took longer, but it definitely helped me in the big picture. I was able to balance the theory of school against the practical application because I could immediately apply what I was learning in the real-world setting of my day job.

From the day I started at Marshall Field's in 1991, I have never stopped working. While I was still in graduate school, I was fortunate to be promoted to the role of Director of Community Relationships for the three department stores that Target, our parent company, owned: Marshall Field's, Dayton's, and Hudson's. Hudson's was based in Detroit, Marshall Field's was in Chicago, and Dayton's was in Minneapolis. My role was to consolidate those three programs into one for greater efficiency and impact. It was an incredible opportunity that would be the kind of job I expected to get after I finished grad school. I was excited, but torn because I wanted to finish my program. I had a year of graduate school left but decided it was too good an opportunity to pass up. In the middle of grad school, I ultimately decided to move to Minneapolis and take the assignment. A year later, I was asked to pick up a part of the Target business and was named director of the Target Foundation. All the while, I was commuting back and forth between Minneapolis and Chicago to finish graduate school. It was really important for me to get my master's and finish graduate school. My great-grandmother's words of wisdom never left me, and those are the values that were entrenched in me. I was going to finish grad school if it took me ten years.

Getting my master's degree definitely helped me with the financial burden of the student loans I had from undergrad. Once I was offered the bigger job and made more money at my company, I could make a commitment to pay off all of my loans before I turned forty. Doing this would require some lifestyle adjustments because I needed to save more money to pay down my loans. My boyfriend (now my husband) and I had to talk about how that would impact both of us. Even though we weren't married yet, it became a family decision. We needed to be together on what we would do as a family to manage our finances. We also realized there might be sacrifices in the moment, but in the long haul they would make it possible for us to live the life we wanted, pay off my loans, and still have money left that we could give charitably. We created a budget that included all of that, so we were able to make that happen.

One piece of advice I offer to young people is to remember that the job and the career that you want to find yourself in may not even exist today. Most of you reading this likely have some type of smartphone. Ten years ago, the technology that we all take for granted today didn't exist. Some of the brands and companies have created industries, economic opportunities, and careers that didn't exist until recent years. We expect the career or industry to already be here and yet in this world—the hyperconnected and fast-paced world in which we live—opportunities are still being created. So, maybe your dream career is waiting for you to create it. That's why it is so important to understand what you want to learn and do to contribute. You need to be nimble, flexible, innovative, curious, adaptive, and resilient and translate your skill and expertise into whatever form exists today or is yet to come. If there is white space and a gap that isn't being filled, that's where you can step in to create and invent the space. Think about the career that you might have tomorrow instead of the job you can have today. That is a different way to frame your future career and life's impact.

I was glad I decided to take the job in Minneapolis because it enabled me to be at the right place at the right time. When the door was opened, I was able to walk through it. It was the right trade-off for me because it led to the next opportunity.

Today, I am the president of Community Relations, where my team and I lead the campaign for education. We give back 5 percent of our profit to the communities in which we operate, and that is an extraordinary commitment, considering that the national corporate average is 1 percent. Target was built on an amazing family value that started with our company and has continued to this day. The things I believe I have done well have happened because I have been a part of an extraordinary team of wicked smart, creative, passionate, brilliant people. They do the work with me, which makes my career and my role to be the bridge between the business and the community possible.

Darren Hardy

"There are no more excuses. If you are still waiting for something to happen, it's on you. Go after it and never look back."

COLLEGE ATTENDED: School of Hard Knocks
OCCUPATION: Publisher, *Success* magazine

A couple of years ago, Darren Hardy tweeted a statistic that really caught my attention. He wrote, "3 million kids graduating and 2.4 of them will be moving home with their parents." I happen to be one of those 2.4 million. His tweet got me curious about why the publisher of *Success* magazine—a man who has spent time with and has interviewed the greatest achievers of our world today, including Richard Branson, Warren Buffett, Bill Gates, Howard Schultz, and just about everyone else on the planet—was tweeting about college graduates.

I thought Darren would be a fantastic resource, but I had no idea just how much I would learn from our conversation. Speaking with Darren was like getting a crash course in reality and what to expect coming out of college while preparing yourself for the future. Darren got me looking at the dilemma that college graduates face in a whole new way by simplifying the process of discovering what you are good at by identifying your strengths and weaknesses and what comes naturally to you. A lot of people I talked to refer to the idea of finding your passion and then following it. He turned that idea into something much broader to think about by taking it beyond "what" it is and thinking about the "how, why, and who" elements too. I had never even thought of finding your passion in that way, and hearing this allowed me to think about my passion from a whole new perspective.

So many people graduate from college believing they can close the chapter on learning and education, but the reality is that this is when the real education of life begins. Darren talked to me about the idea of having to unlearn what you've learned in school and erase the basic principles you were taught because the real world is operating on a newer and more progressive system. When I heard him say this, I immediately had a sense of panic.

"WTF! Erase my mind of what I just spent so many years of my life learning?"

Taking full responsibility for your life is an important concept. So often, people use excuses to validate why they are in a certain situation. We all go through life doing things we think are necessary to facilitate moving things forward, but looking back we rarely ask what we *didn't do*. If you are going to be 100 percent responsible for your life, you have to take responsibility for why you are or are not in the place you want to be.

I have never been the type of person to blame

others for why I am not where I want to be in my life. You can't sugarcoat things when it comes to plotting the course of your future. If you do, you become an enabler, allowing someone else—or worse, yourself—to believe that your excuses are valid and real when they are really just intentional roadblocks. This may sound harsh, but it's true.

When I went to school, I had to work three times harder than the other kids in my class to get the same A as they did. I was a bright kid, but school wasn't really my thing. What I was lacking in passion, I made up for in hard work, discipline, and consistency, three things that will beat out mediocrity every time. I went to college but stayed for only one semester. I got the entrepreneurial bug and wanted to get out into the world to leave my mark. I was nineteen years old when I quit college and had been working for a sales and marketing company selling environmental products door-to-door. I liked what I was doing, which meant I was good at it. The owners of the company were a husband-and-wife team who were going through a divorce. We worked out an arrangement where I could buy the business from them on an earn-out, allowing me to own it without paying any money up front. I built the business up into a five-million-dollar company. I was barely twenty years old, making six figures. By the time I was twenty-four, I was earning seven figures, and by age twenty-seven, my company was worth fifty million dollars. I wonder what two semesters of college would have given me?

My dad was a university football coach who raised me as a single father. His view of the world was that the doctors and lawyers sat at the top of the totem pole, and he also wanted me to strive to be on the top. Being a doctor was out because it wasn't my thing, so I thought I'd become a lawyer. The reality is, I am an anticonformist and a rule breaker. I can't stand people who claim they are a victim or who can't take responsibility and think suing someone will fix their problems. Anyone can tell you that these are not great qualities to become a successful lawyer. It would have been a painful career choice. Luckily, I found something I was passionate about and made it evident that I was really good at it. Sales came naturally to me, and so did running a business. Thankfully, my dad had enough wisdom to notice that I was good at what I was doing. He let it be okay for me to take a pause from college to see if I could make my business work. He told me to give it a go. If it didn't pan out, I could always go back to school. Luckily, I was in a business that played to my strengths. I was seeing momentum with it, so I never looked back. It has been a wild ride ever since.

We are coming out of an entire age in which the culture and society is going through a massive transition. We have come out of the industrial age, in which the workforce was defined by building economic entities, with people performing narrow, repetitive tasks in structured environments, with set controls and capital leveraged through pyramids of hierarchy with clear guidelines. Today, financial capital is no longer the key asset. It is human capital. Success is no longer about economic competence as the main leverage. It is about emotional intelligence. It is no longer about controls. It is about collaboration. It is no longer about hierarchies. It is about leading through networks. It is no longer about aligning people through structures and spreadsheets. It is about aligning them through meaning and purpose. It is no longer about developing followers. It is about developing leaders.

What does all of this mean?

The industrial age is done—dead.

You may be wondering how all of this relates back to you. Here's how. Fifty-four percent of college graduates who have gotten a higher education and put themselves in debt don't have a job. Twenty-seven percent are working in jobs below their education, which means their education has nothing to do with the job they have. And their median income is $27,000 a year. What a lot of people aren't saying is that these jobs are not coming back. Companies have found a way to do more with less. They have outsourced work overseas and created contract workers instead of employees. So even if workers are still performing the same task, they are now sole proprietors. They have become entrepreneurs who need to find other clients to make the same amount of money they used to make working for a single company.

All of this sounds dire, like it is bad news. Think of it like this: If you look back in time, there used to be these big animals called dinosaurs roaming the earth. Then they became extinct. It sounds terrible unless you are a lion. The smaller animal has a chance to thrive and flourish. That's what is happening now. The big corporations and institutions that were the thrust of the industrial age are dying, and they are not coming back. That's a bad thing for the dinosaur but not the lion. Unless you are a small-business owner or a sole proprietor, now is your time to flourish. You are the lion.

A massive economic shift is taking place between the few at the top of the ivory towers who used to have all of the control and those who have broken away from the traditional path. The industrial age was about control of access to the market, which means they controlled the shelves in the stores, the airwaves, information and education, and pretty much everything you wanted access to. All of that is gone now. There is no more control. Everyone has direct access today. Every single person has access to a global marketplace at their fingertips because under those fingertips is a keyboard. There is an enormous opportunity, unprecedented in human history. It is an extraordinary time to be a young person if you learn the skills of entrepreneurship.

Unfortunately, the degree and education that you worked for is probably useless, except for the fact that college taught you to learn. Perhaps college helped you grow up and mature too. But if you think that is done, and now you get to go out into the real world and start making lots of money, you're wrong. You will spend the first three to five years after college trying to unlearn the traditional ideas you were taught. Why? Because most universities still operate under the industrial age mechanisms. Some have tried to adapt and offer some relevant courses, but they are still being taught by people who have the same mentality of the old economic system. Fifty years from now you will look back on your college days and realize what a different era you were in. But for now, you are still bringing your legacy and perspective to your current situation. That is why now is the time to reeducate and get the skills necessary to become a sole proprietor.

What does this really mean?

I am talking about having sole responsibility for your income and being a sole business owner. That is the idea of entrepreneurship. If that means you end up growing a small business or seeing yourself as a contract worker, you will have the necessary skills to contribute something of value. It means you will look for contract work in half a dozen places, make your own schedule, manage your clientele, and dictate your income potential. This is the new world, and no one is better equipped to take advantage of this opportunity than the people in your generation.

The first thing you will need to do to embrace this new reality is wake up to the fact that this is how it is. Your real learning starts now as you develop your skills and character, your emotional resilience, and your emotional intelligence. You will need to develop your social and business aptitude as well. I have never been formally trained for anything I have ever done in my career. I had no business being in business. I had no prior experience. I got in and figured things out.

You have to establish what your strengths are. What are you good at? What comes naturally to you that others struggle with doing? You need to find your passion and the thing you love to do. Finding it is a skill, an attribute, an insight, and an intuitiveness that makes you feel good. For most people, you will usually like doing what you're good at. Let's face it, no one likes doing something they suck at, right? When you find that thing, the whole world opens up, and you will be able to leverage that skill to make the greatest impact.

I was good at taking a complicated situation and quickly getting to the bottom line. I see the basics and the essence of a convoluted situation and can figure out a swift and reasonable resolution. My other strength is my ability to communicate, whether it is speaking to a large crowd at a business conference, talking to someone face-to-face, or writing. In my career path, I have gone from selling environmental products door-to-door, to selling real estate, to building a television network. I have built a national and international distributor force and trained them to perpetuate the install base, done a turnaround of an educational software company, built an Internet business, built another television network, and then became the publisher of *Success* magazine, as well as being an author and a speaker. It may look like all of those jobs have little or nothing to do with one another because they are wildly different industries that appear unrelated, but the one thing in common is my strengths, especially my ability to communicate effectively. These traits were worth money to someone else.

Your waking adult life is going to be spent in what you do professionally, so you'd better like the journey and not just aim for the destination. So how do you find your passion? I have defined four ways to help you get there. It isn't only about loving what you do, although that's one way to get there. The other way is to find the "what," "how," "why," and "who" about whatever it is you're passionate about.

What: "I love what I am doing. This is my passion and what I am good at."

How: "I love how I do this. I want to bring a level of excellence to my work." This is all about how you apply yourself. Are you filled with passion and excitement to go to·work every day, or do you loathe getting out of bed with an overwhelming feeling of dread?

Why: "I love why I am doing this." You are pursuing a mission and a cause that fills your heart even when the day-to-day gets tedious. You stay the course because this is your passion.

Who: "I am doing this for me, not my parents, my boss, or my spouse." This means you are secure in the what, how, and why of your field of work.

If you can't figure out these four things right away, stop using that as an excuse to do nothing. To me, that's a cop-out. Figure out another pathway that is going to ignite your inner fire. It doesn't have to be the process of what you do Monday through Friday, hour by hour. It could be other activities, such as volunteering your time, traveling on a mission, giving back to your community, or helping disadvantaged kids. The possibilities are endless and always worthwhile.

David McClelland, an American psychological theorist, once said that the greatest indicator of someone's success is their reference group, the people they spend the most amount of time with. That's why it is important to surround yourself with the highest level of associations. You become the average of the five people you hang around most. Who are the five people you spend the most time with personally, professionally, and socially? Write down their names and then ask yourself these questions about each one: Is this person taking me in the direction that I want to go? Are they helping? Are they pulling me forward? Or are they dragging me down? If it appears they are neutral, doing neither, cross them off the list. Find five people who are traveling at the pace that you want your life to go.

The influence of association is extraordinary. You will talk about what they talk about and go to the same movies they go to. You will eat in the same restaurants, and generally have the same circle of influencers. As a result, you become an amalgamation of the people you associate with. You have to be conscious about who they are and proactive in putting people into your environment who are going to pull you into the direction you want to go rather than drag you in the direction you don't.

Focus on what you control in life, and don't give any

time or energy to the things you can't. You have to learn to control the controllables and let go of the noncontrollables in life. If you get caught up in paying attention to and being consumed by the world, you are not going to change it by only observing. But it will change how you view things, and therefore, your behavior, activity, and results.

It's time for you to take 100 percent responsibility for your life. Many of you may believe that you already do, but think about how many times you blamed someone or something for things not going your way this week as the reason you are where you are right now.

If you are not working yet, that is your choice.

If you have created debt, that is your choice.

You are responsible for how you respond to everything that is done to you. No matter what circumstance I have faced throughout my career, I always ask myself, "What did I do to create the environment that caused this to happen?" Usually, it boils down to action or inaction as the response.

In all circumstances and in all economies, you are 100 percent responsible. Knowing this is incredibly freeing. It is powerful to understand that you don't have to wait for the "right" time, place, job, market, economy, or any other outside influence to start living your best life. There are no more excuses. If you are still waiting for something to happen, it's on you. Go after it and never look back.

Alli Webb

"Have the confidence to go out and pursue what you want and not what your parents want you to do."

COLLEGE ATTENDED: Florida State University; Fashion Institute in Fort Lauderdale

OCCUPATION: Founder, Drybar

Alli Webb is a woman I admire for taking an idea she believed so strongly in and then running with it. I first met Alli when I was a teenager; I walked past her first store in Brentwood, California, and thought I had found the answer to my prayers. I never got my hair done when I was a teenager unless it was for a special occasion such as prom or semiformal because spending sixty to eighty dollars on a blowout seemed ridiculous. I was always trying to figure out a way to get my hair done without blowing a ton of money. When I walked by the grand opening of Drybar that day, I stopped in to see what the new cool-looking salon was all about. The décor was white and crisp looking with bright yellow accents. There were balloons everywhere, champagne, little treats, and a romantic comedy playing on a large-screen

TV. It felt like such a happy place. Alli was inside with several others, welcoming women as they came in off the sidewalk. She explained the concept to me: quick and affordable blowouts for thirty-five dollars.

"What a perfect idea!" I thought.

When my mom came to pick me up from the shopping center later that day, I couldn't wait to tell her about my new discovery.

My mom loves a strong woman entrepreneur, so we went back in and booked an appointment—for both of us. Knowing how great women feel having their hair done gave Alli the idea to take that knowledge and make it accessible for all women by giving them a deal. And because of that, I knew Alli's business was going to be a huge success.

From the moment you walk through the door, you feel like you are being pampered, and who doesn't want to feel special, especially at such an affordable price? Ever since I walked into that store opening years ago, I have loved watching Drybars pop up all over the country. I feel so proud of Alli and all she has accomplished, especially having taken a nontraditional approach to her education. She attended two separate vocational schools with very different focuses. Realizing early on that traditional schooling wasn't for her and spending her early twenties job-hopping turned out to be an asset to Alli because she had experience in so many different fields, including fashion, beauty, and PR, by the time she launched her own company. She also had the unwavering support of her family, which gave her the confidence to follow her love of making women feel great after a blow-dry—which turned into the dream she had always held close to her heart. She's changing women's lives one blow-dry at a time!

When I graduated from high school, I went down the traditional path that my friends were on and headed off to start my freshman year at Florida State. I remember being in class during my first semester asking myself over and over, "What am I doing here?" I had no idea what I wanted to be, and I felt lost. I was taking some meteorology classes that I thought were cool and interesting, but I had no real passion for the subject. I did a lot of soul-searching that year, wondering what I really should do with my life.

I always had an interest in fashion and had worked in retail at my parents' clothing store. Their parents also owned a clothing store, so it sort of felt like a natural progression for me to follow in my family's footsteps. While I knew I didn't have the artistic skill to become a designer, I thought it would be fun to figure out what I could do in the fashion industry that might pique my interest. I quickly realized that traditional college wasn't for me, and I left Florida State to enroll in the Fashion Institute in Fort Lauderdale.

During my two years at the Fashion Institute, I learned a lot about textiles and fabrics and how the retail business worked, from setting up and running a store to understanding the importance of marketing. When I graduated, I got a job working for fashion designer Nicole Miller as a saleswoman in her Soho store in New York. It was a lucky twist of fate that my brother, Michael, was also working for Nicole Miller at the time, which is how I actually got my foot in the door straight out of college. I had high aspirations to move up the company ladder as fast as I could, becoming the assistant manager shortly after I started.

By the time I was twenty-one, Michael and I had moved back to Florida to open two Nicole Miller boutiques in Miami and Boca Raton. By this time, I had earned the autonomy to be running my own shops. This was also the first time my brother and I actually worked together, which was difficult. We had always been very close, but I was in over my head running the two shops, and the pressure took a definite toll on our relationship. I spent a couple of years being unhappy about what I was doing, especially arguing with my brother all of the time. So I made the sudden and unexpected decision to quit and go to beauty school.

Aside from fashion, I had always had a passion for hair because mine was so difficult to manage. I have naturally curly, frizzy, and wavy hair that I hated and, therefore, preferred to wear blown straight out. Ever since I was a little girl, I somehow felt more pulled together and confident when my hair was blown straight. I was constantly irritated with having to blow-dry my hair all of the time, whether it fell to my mom to do when I was a little girl or to me as I got older. In high school, I'd wash and dry my hair the night before class so I could sleep on it, making it look even smoother. Believe it or not, for someone with super curly or wavy hair, second-day hair always looks a little better than a fresh blowout when you do it yourself. By the time I was sixteen years old I was working as a receptionist in a hair salon, and I remember loving the atmosphere and the energy of the stylists who worked there. Looking back, this might have been where the seed of the idea to do something in hair styling was first planted. It became a deep passion that would take some time to manifest, but I always knew there was a reason I felt so connected to the idea.

I wanted to go to beauty school because my big-picture plan was to learn how to style hair and go back to New York, where I could work on fashion shows and do editorial work. In my mind, that merged my inherent interests in fashion and beauty. I visualized myself as having a huge future career in hair—though I had no idea how that would come to pass. When I shared my idea with my brother, he fully supported my dream because he saw the vision as being the right path for me.

I enrolled in a local beauty school in south Florida and also started working for a friend's dad who owned a local salon. I ended up doing hair in the salon the entire time I was in beauty school and loved it. I was in my early twenties and thought I had found the one thing I was excited about doing every single day. I worked at that salon for three years, gaining valuable experience and dreaming of moving to New York to pursue my grander dream. When I finally got to New York, I had my eye on going to work for John Sahag, a stylist in New York who had a giant celebrity following and who pioneered dry cutting. I was lucky enough to meet him and have John hire me to work in his salon. He was an amazing man and a great mentor. His salons were very Zen, with his two greyhounds lying around when he was doing his haircuts, making it feel comfortable and homey—a perfect environment for me to create in.

Working with John was like going to haircutting boot camp. His approach to hair was nontraditional, so in a way, I had to relearn everything they taught me in beauty school. His philosophy was that you see the hair differently when it is dry as opposed to wet. That was his process and one that I spent a couple of years learning and perfecting before I once again decided it was time to move on.

I was young, so even though a lot of people may look at my bouncing around as a time in my life when I wasn't settled or committed, I saw it as the only time that I had the flexibility to figure out what I really wanted to do with my life. Even though I was always working, the "What's next?" question persisted in the back of my mind for years.

After working with hair for a couple of years, the truth is I wasn't challenged by it anymore. I had a friend who was working for a PR company in New York who was always going to really fun parties and events meeting all sorts of interesting people from celebrities to business leaders to New York City socialites. It seemed like she was having so much more fun than I was, so I took a job working as an assistant at their PR firm. I was working under someone who represented Faith Hill, Tim McGraw, and Jennifer Lopez, which I thought was pretty cool. But the job wasn't a walk in the park. It required a lot of skills I hadn't expected. Out of necessity, I learned to sharpen my writing during this time because a big part of my job required me to create compelling press releases and communicate with the media. I also learned a lot about composing myself and being professional in that environment because I had only worked in fashion and hair prior to joining the PR firm. Stylists and fashion people can get away with being a little kooky in their appearance and behavior, but publicists have to be far more refined.

Even though my path appeared to be random and all over the board, it was *my* path. Each experience offered me amazing opportunities for learning valuable lessons. It also brought me to meeting my husband. A year after we met, we got married. I decided I wanted to have kids right away and be a stay-at-home wife and mom. We moved to Los Angeles and set up our home and life, while my husband pursued his career in advertising. While we probably should have spent a little more time traveling and enjoying each other's company, I was eager to start having kids. I gave birth to my first son in 2005. When I became a first-time mom, I immersed myself in the world of being a mommy: going to mommy support groups, Mommy-and-me classes, Music Together—you name it, I was there. I was like a hippie mom whose kid was always attached to me. I was great at it and genuinely loved where my life had taken me. By the time I had my second son in 2007, I began feeling like I needed to get out of the house more and do some things on my own. I was getting antsy and didn't feel like I could go to the park one more day. It felt like my brain had dried up because I wasn't doing anything to contribute to society.

Since my parents were entrepreneurs, that spirit definitely ran through my blood. I had the itch to get back out there, and this time I wanted to start my own business. At this point, I had thirteen years of experience doing other people's hair. All of my friends knew I could blow out hair really well and they would frequently ask me to do theirs. I was sitting in my living room one afternoon talking to my best friends when I said, "What if we started a business where I would just blow-dry our friends' hair in their homes and charge something like thirty-five or forty dollars to do it." At the time, the idea of someone coming to your home for a blow-dry was a super expensive proposition. I knew women who were spending hundreds of dollars for that service. Surely there was a market of moms out there who would jump on board if I kept my prices affordable. There was really only one way to test the market, and that was to post an entry on a local mommy blog called Peach Head, a website that reached five thousand moms in the Los Angeles area. I had been using it for mommy stuff and thought it was a great resource. My post read something like this:

"I am thinking about starting a mobile blow-dry business where all I do is blow-dry hair. I will come to your house and charge $35–$40 cash. What do you think?"

I was inundated with positive e-mails.

Before I knew it, I was spending my entire day driving around Los Angeles, blow-drying as many women as I could squeeze in while juggling my mom duties at home. As a result of the rapid successful response, I had to start saying no to people because I didn't have enough hours in a day to fit everyone in. I didn't want to turn away the business, and at the time, there was only one stylist— me—and I couldn't be in more than one place at a time. Whenever I turned away a customer, I was curious about what they would do. So I started to ask. They told me they would go to a local salon where they would pay a lot more money or don a large pair of black sunglasses and sneak into a discount salon chain hoping no one would see them. While they might be getting decent enough blowouts, I knew that the experience of going to those chain salons wasn't what they wanted or were used to, because I felt that way too whenever I did the same thing. It dawned on me that I once had the same problem they did.

That was when the lightbulb came on. There was a hole in the market for a comfortable, affordable salon that specialized in hair-washing and blow-dry service. No haircuts, no color, just blowouts. That was when the idea for Drybar began to emerge.

Unlike other salons, Drybar would make money by maximizing the volume of customers we could see in a single day. Blowouts don't take as much time in the chair as color or cuts. It was strictly a numbers game. If we could do enough blowouts a day, I was positive we could make money. I remember laying in bed thinking to myself, "If five people come in an hour and we are open for ten hours a day, that's fifty people and I could make that work." Anything less would be a disaster.

Launching a business is completely an all-encompassing, all-consuming effort. Getting any business off the ground takes an unprecedented amount of dedication, focus, and sheer will. Having a great idea is one thing, but pulling together the thousands of little details necessary to bring that idea to reality is another story. It took a solid six months of "high burn" where everyone involved, including my brother, my husband, my sister-in-law, our architect and partner Josh Heitler, and me, were spending just about every waking hour, seven days a week, working on Drybar.

Our efforts covered architecture and design, branding, marketing, computer systems, and public relations—not to mention finding and training dozens and dozens of stylists. When we had all of the elements in place, despite my brother's initial concerns about how we'd turn a profit, he believed in my idea so much that he gave me the initial startup capital to launch. He would probably say he didn't really expect to see that money again, but he believed in me and my ability to pull it off.

My first location was at an outdoor shopping center in Brentwood, California. Once we opened our first shop, it took everything we had just to keep the doors open. It was complete chaos in those early days, but it was also more fun than you can imagine—it was such a bonding experience for us all, and it laid the foundation for our culture and values in years to come.

When we opened our doors for business, people came in raving about the idea, often sharing how regretful they were that they didn't think of it first. Many even said they had thought about doing the same thing but never followed through. Having a good idea is only part of the equation to success. You also need to have the courage, passion, and dedication to execute it. When you feel passionate about something, it isn't work—it's a dream come true.

When I look back on the paths that led me to starting Drybar, I never would have mapped it out the way it unfolded. I don't feel like I am a huge success. Yes, I have been successful, but I still believe I have a lot more left to do. Still, there's nothing quite like having a woman I've never met tell me that somehow, the time she spends in our salons has changed her life. I often joke that we are changing the world one blowout at a time, which I know is a little lofty, and yet it is amazing the impact this seedling of an idea has had on women all over the country. It gives them confidence and helps them feel up after having a down day, and in the process we have opened twenty-six locations in six states, doing 50,000 blowouts a month. We have also created more than fifteen hundred jobs in just a little over three years in business. I still worry that people won't come into the salons before a grand opening. I don't think that will ever go away.

Adam Braun

"When evaluating a potential job, usually one will be a better experience and one will pay you more money. You will learn more from the better experience. There is a time and place to choose money over a learning environment, but you do that when the margin is very big, and that doesn't happen right out of school."

COLLEGE ATTENDED: Brown University, bachelor's degree in economics, sociology, and public and private sector organizations

OCCUPATION: Founder and CEO, Pencils of Promise

Before interviewing Adam Braun, I didn't know much about him except that he had started an amazing organization. When a friend of mine told me his story, I knew it would be great to share in this book. His stories of traveling around the world and seeing things that we take for granted every day that so many people aren't able to have left him figuring out a way to give those in developing countries something as simple as a pencil. Adam understood that merely providing children with the opportunity to write something down on a piece of paper made all the difference in the quality of their education, as well as their ability to express themselves. It hadn't occurred to me that something so basic symbolized such a powerful tool of self-discovery. It takes a lot of bravery to travel around the world alone, and I respect the time Adam gave himself to look inward and discover what he really wanted to do with his life after college.

I found myself relating to his story because I've spent some time traveling to places like Africa and seeing the depths of poverty that are unimaginable to most of us unless you experience it firsthand. In 2010, I took my first trip to Ghana to visit maternity wards with my uncle and the ONE Foundation. While I was there, I saw what ONE and (RED) had done to raise money to build a maternity ward and testing center where women could get tested for HIV and deliver their babies with the proper medical attention and medication to survive. I have never been able to get that experience out of my mind. I am so used to going to the hospital to visit friends or family after they have a baby where the hospital is clean, sometimes fancy, and where the mother is in a bed with nurses and doctors tending to her around the clock.

The "maternity ward" I saw in Africa couldn't have been more different from what we see at home. It was essentially two boxy concrete buildings that had a line of women waiting outside. One was where women and men could get tested for HIV, and the other was where women delivered their babies. Outside that structure, some of the women were dressed in regular clothes waiting to have their babies, while others were wearing just hospital gowns, sitting outside in the rows of seats holding babies that had just been born. I was told that women walk for miles to come to this hospital because hospitals with that kind of medical care are rare. It looked like an assembly line of pregnant women going in, having their babies, and then being sent on their way. After experiencing that, I wanted to do more to help bring awareness to the issues women around the world deal with that most of us would consider unimaginable. I understand the frustration of discovering an issue that exists that we think can be easily fixed, and because of that, I appreciate the unwavering dedication Adam has for his cause.

One of the most important takeaways from my conversation with Adam was his message to be patient. That was hard for me, especially in the months that followed after I graduated. I was frustrated knowing that I wanted to get out and do something so badly but wasn't sure exactly what it was. I had the desire but lacked the patience to allow things to unfold and learn about myself while I was still figuring it all out. I think many of us have grown up in an age where everything is instantaneous, so when we want something, for the most part, we can get it. Being patient is hard, but I've learned that if I am patient, answers always come.

When I was a student at Brown University, I went on the Semester at Sea program, where I met a young boy begging on the street in India. He told me that all he wanted was a pencil, so I handed him mine. I was twenty-one years old when I experienced that exchange, and I knew I would eventually start a global education organization to help other kids like that boy. After meeting him, I made it a point to pass out pencils to children throughout my travels all over the world. A pencil may seem simple and unimportant to us, but for children living in impoverished conditions, it is a tool for self-discovery and education. That was the impetus for what became Pencils of Promise, though I didn't start the nonprofit organization right away. In my mind, I didn't have the means to start it yet. I figured I would get a job, work twenty years, save enough money, and then start a great organization.

Although I was offered a job at a prestigious management consulting firm right out of college, I decided to spend a year traveling around the world. Back then, firms like the one I was hired at paid signing bonuses for accepting a job with their company. They gave me $10,000 to say yes. I knew in my heart that this was the only time in my life that I didn't need to know what was coming next. I took my signing bonus and decided to backpack around the world, eventually visiting more than fifty countries and igniting my deep interest in international development. When you are twenty-three years old, traveling through the developing world by yourself provides a lot of time for self-reflection. Although I had direction in my life, I still felt lost. That sense of not knowing what was coming next ate away at me. Even though I knew I had a job lined up, I didn't really know what I wanted to do for a career.

When I returned from my year sabbatical, I went to work in corporate America at the management consulting firm in New York City.

By the time I started at the firm, I was clear with everyone that I was there to learn as much as I could before starting a nonprofit organization that would impact global education one day. I looked at my time there as paid business school. I knew what I wanted to do next and just needed to figure out how to get there.

In late September 2008, I went to the Philharmonic in New York City. I had never been to the symphony before and didn't know what to expect. At one point in the program, a man came out onto the stage and played an unforgettable piece on the piano. It impacted me greatly, and I wanted to be as passionate about something as he was about his instrument. The scene on stage made me reassess my true passion in life. Sitting in the audience at the Philharmonic that night watching the gifted pianist, I acknowledged there was more I could be doing to give back to others. Suddenly, the name "Pencils of Promise" came to me in that moment, and I couldn't escape my desire to start a charity with the aim of building small schools in developing countries. I knew this was where I could make the biggest difference.

I went home from the symphony that night and wrote out the initial charter and every idea I could think of to launch. I wanted to build a school in honor of my grandmother, who was a Holocaust survivor. I had a need to find a way to honor her because she had sacrificed the most so I could be in the position I was in. Ten days later, I took my mission statement to the bank and asked them what I would need to do to start an account for my new charity. They said I could open the account with a $25 deposit, so I put that money into the bank. I was about to turn twenty-five that month too. Instead of having a big party where all of my friends and family came with needless gifts, I threw a birthday party to raise my initial funds for Pencils of Promise.

It took several months to get the nonprofit registered and operational. The company I was working for had an externship program where I could take a six-month leave of absence and work for someone else. Although there was an approved list of companies you could go to, I went to my boss and explained that I wanted to do something entrepreneurial. In the end, he agreed to let me do it.

Just as I left my job, the economy began to tank. It was a challenging time to start a charity because people were tightening their belts, not opening their wallets. Since my externship was unpaid and because of the state of the economy at the time, my bosses extended my sabbatical from six to nine months, so I didn't have to worry about having a job to come back to if my new venture didn't work out as I had hoped. Despite the odds, and through a few more small fund-raising events, we were able to raise enough money to build the first school in Southeast Asia. When I came back, I took the rest of my time to tour the United States in an RV and speak at colleges, sharing my experiences with the hope of inspiring other young people to do something with their lives that fulfilled them and gave their work meaning.

I returned to my management consulting job in late 2009. I was trying to balance both worlds, juggling my day job in finance with my passion for philanthropy. My time away was meant to be an opportunity to learn and grow so I could come back to my position at the firm with more experiences and greater insights to help me in my job. Instead, it showed me that I wasn't where I really wanted to be, so in March 2010, I decided to pursue Pencils of Promise full time.

Once Pencils of Promise became a full-time venture, I was never more grateful for my triple major in college in economics, sociology, and public and private sector organizations (PPSOs). Those three were the perfect intersection that enabled me to make the charity successful. Economics was helpful to understand how capital flows and the relevance of general economic theories in the real world (yes, they matter!). I was most interested in sociology because I have always been fascinated with what motivates people, how people move collectively, and how revolutions occur. And finally, the PPSO major taught me the basics of being an entrepreneur and how nonprofits and for-profits work. I took classes in leadership, creating effective business plans and more practical information than theoretical ideas. Together, these three disciplines helped me craft a strong professional career with a foundation laid through my experiences in college and the years that followed. I am also grateful for the time I spent working in corporate America and am a big proponent of it. I think you should go to work for the best company you can before trying to start your own. Sure, there are examples of people who were able to make a business work on their own, but I believe there is no replacement for the practical and formal experience you gain working for someone else who is really good at what they do. It doesn't have to be for years, but you won't regret the time you spend learning from people who have been through the process before you.

Since I left the world of finance, I have worked harder than I ever have in my life, but I don't feel that I am doing hard work. I am not doing something I hate or resent— I am doing the work I love.

Maria Shriver

"Work hard, be lucky, be awake, and never think you are too good to do x, y, and z."

COLLEGE ATTENDED: Georgetown University, bachelor's degree in American Studies

OCCUPATION: Journalist, author, activist, mother

I decided to interview my mom for this book because I think her story of transitioning into life after college is relatable, honest, and one that a lot of people can learn from. Plus, she is my mom and for the most part, I've grown up hearing her stories and learning from them, so I wanted to pass her knowledge on to you. Even though I went into the interview with an exceptional amount of information, I found myself wanting to know more.

My mom has always spoken to me about the never-ending cycle of the "Now what?" question. What I didn't know was that she went through the very same feeling of not knowing what she was going to do when she graduated from Georgetown. I was surprised when she shared that she told people she was thinking of going to law school just to get them off her back. I laughed when I heard this because it was very similar to what I was doing when I told people I was just "pausing."

My mom and I have an unusual thing in common—we both come from well-known families. While some people might think this opens doors and gets you preferential treatment (and sometimes it does), it can also work against you. When my mom was starting out, people often said to her, "I bet you got the job because of your family," and then they would follow it up with, "By the way, which Kennedy are you?" Even her first boss told her to her face that the only reason she was in his newsroom was because of her last name.

Her experiences dealing with a famous last name have helped me deal with mine. Everyone wants to be accepted for who they are, and not for who their parents are or for whom they're related to. I don't think you have to have a famous last name to understand what I am talking about. You can be the sister of the head cheerleader, the brother of the star quarterback, or the child of a local pediatrician to know what I mean. Everyone wants to carve an individual path and light the world on fire. There is something unique and special in each and every one of us that makes us our own person. What I have learned from my mom is that there is no shortcut to getting where you want to go. No matter what your name is, you have to do the work. Your name may get you in the door, but your talent is what will keep you there.

One of the many things that inspires me about my mom is how she juggled her passion for journalism, her passion for motherhood, and her passion for being a great wife to my dad. Even if she weren't my mom, I would still want to interview her for this book because so many of us want to learn how to juggle many things in our lives and be able to do it well.

Another thing that I respect about my mom is that she gives credit to the village that has helped her get to where she is: her family, my dad, and the people she has worked with along the way. She says that she couldn't have made it without any of them and credits all of them for helping her get to where she is today. My mom always reminds me that you never get anywhere on your own, and that everyone needs support and encouragement.

When it comes to figuring out a plan for your future, my mom always says that no matter how much we all plan out our lives, life can take an unexpected turn. That is why it's really important to try to let go of your plan and accept where you are in the moment and then make the most out of it. She had to change her journalism plan with the birth of each of us kids and had to change it again when my dad ran for governor, and she became First Lady. She always tells my siblings and me to keep evolving, keep learning, and keep moving forward with your head high and your humor in tow.

I am very appreciative of my time at Georgetown University. It forced me to raise my game in terms of my work ethic because it was hard and the stakes were high. Although my major in American Studies didn't really prepare me for a career in journalism, it did help me sharpen my writing skills. Georgetown is where I learned to work really hard. I minored in theology, which not only was something I was interested in but also reiterated the values I had in my life. It helped me strengthen my ethics, which would become helpful in my work. Georgetown represented honesty, integrity, and values that were important to me.

I come from an accomplished family and an accomplished extended family. I have four brothers, and our parents were tough and extremely driven and expected a lot from the five of us. The level of what people accomplished in my family was enormous, and I always worried how I would measure up. The best way to get my parents' attention was to do well in my work.

When I graduated from Georgetown, I knew I wanted to work in television. When I was a senior in high school, I went on the campaign trail with my father, who was running for vice president, and I experienced the journalists covering the campaign firsthand. I spent time with them, watching them work, and I saw their impact.

Aha. That is what I want to do, I thought.

After graduating from Georgetown, I applied to a training program at Westinghouse Broadcasting. If I was accepted, I had no idea where I would live, what city I would go to, or what I'd be doing. Since being in front of the camera and working in television news was my goal, I was willing to do what it took to achieve that. I spent my summer waiting to hear about the training program, feeling anxious and embarrassed about not knowing what I would be doing next. It didn't help that everywhere I went, people were asking, "Do you know what you're going to do?" The honest answer was, "I have no idea." Not having an answer made me feel bad about myself. This insecurity was compounded by the inevitable conversation that followed which went something like this:

"What do you mean, you don't know what you want to do?"

"I don't know. I think I want to work in TV. I'm just trying to figure it out."

"You're going to work in TV? How are you going to do that? Where are you going to live and who is going to hire you?"

"I don't know. It depends if I get accepted into the training program I applied to."

Looking back, I sounded so unclear and lost. It felt like I was the only one who didn't have an answer for what was next. I remembered hearing people confidently talk about what they wanted to do when they got out of college all the way back in high school. A good friend of mine was certain she would be a doctor. Others were certain they would work on Wall Street or in politics. A lot of kids I graduated from college with moved to New York, went to law school, or ended up working on Wall Street as planned.

When I finally received the letter of acceptance into the management training program at Westinghouse, it said I'd be working in Philadelphia. I left twenty-four hours later, partly because I didn't want anyone to ask me what I was doing and partly because I was starting my job right away and needed to find a place to live. When I got to Philadelphia, I moved into a hotel until I could find an apartment. I didn't know a single person when I got there except a guy I went to college with who lived outside the city.

The training program was designed to take you through all the different departments of a local TV station. When you arrive, they ask what area you want to focus on. For me it was news, but first, the program took me through sales and then marketing. Finally I was placed in the newsroom, and I couldn't have been happier. Even though my job consisted of getting coffee, logging reporters' tapes, and sitting up all night listening to the police radio, I was still thrilled to be there. Unfortunately, I can't say the same for the news director. He was not only upset that I had been put directly into the newsroom but also outraged that I had been accepted into the training program in the first place. He felt that I didn't need the money or the job and that I was taking up a space of someone who did. Because of this, he tried to break me. He got me to cry one time, and that was it.

Instead of getting discouraged, I was determined to prove him wrong. I wanted to show him that not only could I do the job, but I was worthy of it. It was really important to me to make my own way and make my own name. I grew up as a Kennedy, and in people's minds, we were all the same—we all had big hair and big teeth. I was really motivated to no longer be invisible in this big group. I needed to get out from under that label and prove that

I wasn't some rich kid who had no work ethic. I wanted to be more than just hair and teeth. I wanted to be Maria.

I stuck it out for a year before I was allowed to apply for a job at one of Westinghouse's five other stations. I sent résumés out for every job that was available to me. My hard work paid off and eventually I was offered a writer/producer/sound person job at WJZ-TV in Baltimore. I packed up my car and hit the road.

I loved my new position at WJZ. I was working seven days a week, twelve hours a day, writing and producing news stories. I was also the sound woman on my stories. I didn't know anything about the technical aspects of the position, and I didn't think I'd be able to lift all of that gear or know where to plug anything in. But I learned. Besides, I thought I would earn more respect from the crew and reporters if they saw that I was willing to work my way up through the ranks. I will admit that although I wanted to work on camera, in the beginning, I was too scared. I decided that I would learn all I could behind the scenes, even if that meant holding a boom. The urge to be in front of the camera was growing, but I felt that I had to pay my dues and prove I could do it. Knowing all of the aspects of the job would surely make me a better reporter.

In 1980, I left WJZ to work on the presidential campaign of my uncle, Senator Edward Kennedy. During that time, I think I gained twenty pounds, going from tea party to tea party on his behalf. I think I actually ate my way through Iowa. I was on the road for six months, and it showed. After the campaign ended, I decided to move to

California because I was in a relationship with Arnold Schwarzenegger. We had been dating for three years, and I wanted to be closer to him. When I got settled there, I met with a television news agent and told him about my dream to be on camera. He told me I was too fat to be on TV, and as if that weren't enough, he also said that my voice was irritating. The bottom line was that he wouldn't sign me unless I lost forty pounds and went to a voice coach.

Even though I had done what the agent suggested— lost the weight and worked with the voice coach—and went back to see him, when he sent me out to audition, I couldn't get an on-camera job. But I found a producing position on a news show called *Portrait of a Legend*. It was a show that profiled legends in music. Seeing an opportunity, I asked the lead producer if I could shoot footage of myself interviewing the people I was profiling. I told him he didn't have to put it on the air, but I needed footage to make a reel. Luckily, the producer agreed to let me do that, so I wrote, produced, and interviewed various people for these segments, and he gave me the footage I needed.

Once my reel was complete, I sent it back to Westinghouse Broadcasting, which at the time was syndicating a show called *Evening Magazine*. When I sent my reel, I explained that I had worked as a producer at their Philadelphia and Baltimore stations, and I was now looking to be on camera. They remembered me, liked what they saw, and hired me to be a national correspondent for all of their *Evening Magazine* shows. I traveled all over the world, mainly doing lifestyle and entertainment stories. I had the time of my life. A lot of people started their careers at *Evening Magazine*: Matt Lauer, Leeza Gibbons, Mary Hart, and many more. I got so much experience, and my goal was to anchor a morning show. Secretly, that had always been my dream, but I never spoke about it to anyone because it was such a crazy idea. At the time, there were only three networks, and I thought it would be impossible to become an anchor, though I always wanted to do that.

So, in 1983, I sent my updated reel out to the three networks. *CBS Morning News* was trying to open a larger presence in Los Angeles. They hired me as their local correspondent, covering the West Coast for the network. At the time, Diane Sawyer was the anchor of the show in New York. Eventually, I got to fill in for her a few times when she went on vacation, mostly on Christmas or when nobody else wanted to work.

I vividly remember the first time I sat in for her. I was so nervous that I threw up in the bathroom right before I went on the air. And when the camera went on, I spoke super fast. It wasn't my best work, but I somehow managed to make it through.

When you're in journalism, you are always on call. People work holidays, and that is usually what leads to your big break. If you are curious and want to do your best in a job, that is how you learn the most. It was up to me to make my reputation, book my stories, and find my own beat. It took me a while, but eventually I found my way.

When Diane left *The Morning Show* to do *60 Minutes*, I wanted her job, but I got passed over. The network hired

Phyllis George to replace her. Once again I was the substitute, but I kept on working, and lo and behold, when
Phyllis left abruptly, guess who got her job? Me!

I had just gotten engaged a month before, so I was
nervous about accepting it. Arnold and I discussed it, and
with his encouragement I took the job and moved to New
York. I was proud to be the first woman in morning news
who would get equal pay and equal billing to the male
host. Most important, I also had an equal opportunity with
the stories.

I had the greatest year doing what I loved most. Unfortunately, a year after I was hired, the president of the
network decided to take the show out of the news division
and move it to their entertainment division because he felt
that they would achieve higher ratings. (He was wrong.)
But as a result of his decision, in August 1986, everyone
associated with the show was fired. I was offered a correspondent job at CBS, but I was so mad about the way
things were handled that I said, "No, thank you." I walked
out the door and vowed to myself that I would never walk
back into that building again.

I had gotten married in April that year so when I left
CBS, I moved back to Los Angeles. I was offered a lot of
money to do the local news shows, but that didn't feel
right to me. I had spent a year in local news and I didn't
like sitting behind a desk reporting on murders and plane
crashes. I enjoyed being out, telling stories and meeting
people. As a kid growing up, I loved to read a lot of bi-
ographies. I have always been curious about people and

their stories. I am interested in what makes them tick, how they overcame problems and eventually found their way. I never wanted to be just a news anchor reader; I wanted to be out in the field and I wanted to tell people's stories in a compelling way. That's why I enjoyed morning news—it blends hard and soft news.

I was intrigued when I found out NBC was launching a new newsmagazine show and wanted me for a correspondent position. Even though they offered the least amount of money and a 70 percent pay cut, I thought there was the most room for growth. I had heard rumors that they might also be starting a weekend version of *The Today Show*, and I thought maybe it would lead me back to an anchor role. I took the job and stayed at NBC from 1986 to 2004, anchoring their weekend news, the *Sunday Today* show, and *Dateline*; I substituted on *The Today Show* and I anchored the children's magazine show called *Main Street*. I worked on NBC Sports, covering the Olympics, and I had my own show called *First Person with Maria Shriver*, where I was reporting on people doing interesting and cutting-edge things. Through television, I felt I could influence others about things to think about and take them places they couldn't go on their own.

My secret to becoming a successful journalist is pretty simple. I was passionate, curious, and hungry. Working with someone who inspires you can ignite you. Think of how a teacher ignites a kid into a passion or a love of learning. Who you work for is far more important than what you do. If you can get a low-level job but work for a really inspiring boss, that is better than a high-level job working for a jerk. If you can answer a phone, but you are in a great organization working for someone who has a vision, who is an inspiration, and who wants to do something important, being in that environment ignites you to think and be creative. If you are around people who are working hard and trying to do interesting things, you will find that it raises your game. It's like playing tennis with someone who is better than you—your skills rapidly improve. When you play with someone who can barely hit the ball, you have no motivation. Self-motivation is important, but having someone who takes an interest in you—and it only takes one person—can get you fired up.

When I look back on leaving CBS, I understand that how you leave a job is extremely important. How you behave on the job matters, but how you exit that job is critical. When I left CBS, even though I was mad, I made a conscious choice not to bad-mouth people. I will tell them how I feel in an honest and direct way, but I always do my best to maintain the relationships I worked so hard to build along the way. I have bumped into the people I worked with many times over the years, from executives to members of the crew. I am especially nice to the crew because they can make or break you when you are on camera.

Try to be grateful in your work and to the people who help you. And by all means, stay humble and open. All of those experiences help awaken you and your life to the world around you. Life is about constantly waking up and taking notice.

Matt Barkley

"The real world can be hard at times, but I don't think people are willing to sacrifice enough. . . ."

COLLEGE ATTENDED: University of Southern California, bachelor's degree in communications

OCCUPATION: Quarterback for the Philadelphia Eagles

I first met Matt Barkley in a communications class we took together at USC during my sophomore year of college, and we quickly became friends. Although he had fielded many offers to turn pro during college, I greatly admired Matt's dedication to getting his degree and finishing what he started before moving on to play professional football. Most people would have been tempted to take the big-money deals he was being offered and walk away from their education, but as I got to know Matt through the years, I would come to understand that he is not like most people. He is a man of great strength and character. Because of his strong foundational beliefs and faith and constant positive attitude, Matt is the type of man who will become incredibly successful at his career no matter what he ends up doing after playing professional football.

Matt has so much confidence in his path and is completely secure that everything in his future will turn out great and the way it was meant to be. After finishing college, as expected, Matt went into the NFL draft. When he wasn't drafted in the first round, he was calm and remained positive that his turn would come—and it did. I truly respect that Matt is completely in touch with who he is and has complete trust that God has a bigger plan than our own.

Matt has always been willing to do whatever it took to be the best in everything he does, whether it was training on the field, studying, reviewing footage from his past games, or playing the game he loves so dearly—football. He gives 100 percent of his effort to everything he does. His unwavering dedication is inspiring to me, as is his faith in himself and his capabilities to accomplish whatever he sets out to do.

One of the biggest misconceptions I think college graduates have right out of school is the notion that things will come easy. A lot of people sacrifice their time, maybe working multiple jobs and shifts, to make ends meet for their families, but too many college kids come out of school expecting things to be given to them—especially a job. They expect there to be money in the bank, when they actually have to work for it. It comes as a shock to some that you may have to challenge yourself to reach out and earn that money by making things happen for yourself rather than sitting around waiting for opportunities to be handed to you. I look at it as stepping out of your comfort zone and challenging yourself to go places beyond where you've been. For some, this may mean learning to be humble by doing menial tasks they view as beneath them, while others will have to sacrifice time and location to get what they ultimately want. As I approached graduation, I knew I would have to sacrifice all of the above.

When I graduated from USC, I had no idea let alone any control over where I would be living later that year. My fate was in the hands of a coach someplace out there who might or might not want me to play for his team. I am definitely blessed to make a living playing football in the NFL, but to do so, I would have to give up the security I had growing up in California, being near my family and everything I'd come to feel comfortable around, and move to a new city to start a new life and career. Looking back, juggling academics and athletics was a tough act that was very demanding, but it helped prepare me to handle the demands I would face as a professional athlete. I am blessed to make a living playing a game I love. It's my dream job and all I have wanted and worked for since I was a kid.

I believe in setting high goals, but you have to be willing to work your way up to achieve them. To do this successfully, you have to have a plan. You need to understand what you want—*really* want—and how you are going to execute each step required to get there. A plan isn't just about your career—you need to plan how you are going to handle your finances, your relationships, your family, and other obligations that come your way after college. In my case, I also had to formulate a backup plan in case I get hurt on the field and my football career comes to a sudden and unexpected end. I didn't want to be the guy who worked my entire life toward one goal and have nothing to fall back on, so I studied communications in college because being a sports commentator has always been an interest of mine. If and when my pro career ends, I would place all of my attention on pursuing that goal. I also have a passion for helping the less fortunate, so I know I will continue taking the humanitarian trips I've done all over the world since I was a kid. There's nothing more satisfying than being of service to others and giving back in any way you can.

Cristina Carlino

"Courage requires the ability to fail. If you can't handle failure or being wrong, you will never succeed."

COLLEGE ATTENDED: School of Hard Knocks

OCCUPATION: Founder, Biomedic and Philosophy; founder and executive chair, Archetypes, Inc.

I wanted to interview Cristina Carlino because I have been a huge admirer of her Philosophy brand and products for years. Philosophy is a brand of beauty products that were developed to celebrate the beauty of the human spirit. The products are made with the finest ingredients and are meant to simplify skin care. I knew that Cristina had sold her company and gone through a life-altering transition afterward, and I thought it might be interesting to hear her perspective on what she sacrificed to build her company and what that meant to her along the way. Talking to Cristina was an eye-opening experience because she was the first person I spoke with who explained that when people have high expectations of you, there is inevitably more pressure to perform and do great things out of college.

While I had heard the saying that "life is a class-room" many times before our interview, it had never occurred to me that someone with Cristina's success and experiences would still see the world that way. She still learns something new every day and is eager and excited to stay in the classroom of life. Her insights helped me see that you really do learn so much more about life—*living* your life—than you get in a university setting, especially when you are connected, present, and aware of all of the tremendous possibilities that exist in the real world. What Cristina helped me realize is that *confidence* isn't the secret to success so much as *courage*. Having the *courage* to fail, being able to say we failed, and being willing to open the door to the lessons we learn from failing teaches us far more about life than our successes. You aren't going to get things perfect all of the time, but you can strive to be your very best. And when life presents challenges, see those as learn-ing opportunities and continuing education instead of setbacks.

I read an article in *The New Yorker* about how your high school years define who you are for the rest of your life. From a social standpoint, this was absolutely true for me. I became deeply introverted, uneasy, and self-conscious about myself. I had terrible social anxiety, and when it came to being in new situations, I completely shut down. This unnerving angst led me to decide not to attend college.

I was an excellent student who loved school, but I wasn't a traditional learner, and because of that, failure wasn't a scary thing for me. I never considered myself to be a classic intellectual—as a *true* intellectual is someone who is interested in everything. I am more interested in specific things. For example, I couldn't get my brain to read sheet music, but I could hear music, so I never felt like I couldn't be connected to it. I was also interested in all things medical, so had I gone to college, I am certain I would have gone on to study medicine. But I didn't.

I discovered at a very early age that life is a classroom. You get the best education in everyday experiences when you take the time to absorb what is happening around you. Life is the best teacher, and if you're lucky, your education doesn't end after college—it's just the beginning.

When I told my family that I didn't want to go to college, they wrote me off with the expectation that my life would amount to zero. While some people may have perceived that kind of rejection as negative, I saw it as being lucky. When you are a dark horse, nobody is counting you as a contender in the race. It wasn't that I had extraordinary confidence—I didn't. I don't think anyone ever really has *enough* confidence. Sure, I've felt bad about my decision over the years, and there were plenty of times I was in the room with some highly accomplished people where I wished I'd had a broader knowledge base, but I made up for that insecurity by becoming a woman who worked hard for my entire life and, *despite* other people's doubts, became successful. When high expectations are placed on you because of who you are or what someone else expects you to do, it creates an excessive amount of pressure to succeed. It's a lot easier to reach your goals when you don't have all of that pressure to live up to. When you fall, no one is paying attention. Knowing that early in my career made it a lot easier to pick myself up, brush myself off, and get back in the race.

Philosophy was born out of a person who was seeking. Part of me that believes that there is a master plan that takes us to where we are meant to go, whether you graduate from college or not. You may not use the same steps to get there, but you will most likely end up in the same place if it's meant to be. Since I always had bad skin, the part of me who was always interested in medicine and science began looking at what they were teaching in beauty school. The funny thing about beauty school is that they don't teach doctors—they teach estheticians. Every time I went to see a doctor for my skin, they handed me a prescription for products that left my skin red and raw. Eventually, I would stop using the medication and my skin would remain the same. This is how I became connected to the industry. I knew the problem—so I committed myself to finding a solution. By the time I was twenty-nine years old, I had founded a company called Biomedic, which was about topical skin care products for people with dysfunctional skin. I had no medical degree, but there I was, a person who created a totally medically based topical product line.

Biomedic was a success, but I felt very boxed in by the rules and regulations that go along with good medicine. "You can do this, but not that." The creative part of me wanted to expand beyond those limits. And that is how Philosophy was born. It was created for my own specific likes and dislikes. I didn't like complicated skin care. I loved the way food smelled, so instead of creating a medicinal-smelling, complicated system, I chose to simplify skin care and use fragrances that were appealing and soothing. No one was doing skin care from that point of view, and in the process, I found my passion.

Sometimes you get a feeling in your gut that is so clear it's impossible to ignore. If you don't listen to it, then you may miss some of the most important information you were supposed to have in your life. When you are in a pocket or in the zone, your life moves to a synchronistic place. There are no coincidences. When you are consciously aware of your choices, you are awake to everything you are doing. I spent the first forty-nine years of my life in a drag-along program of creating companies as a way of hiding my pain from the past. When I sold Philosophy, I didn't have work to distract me; I just had myself to deal with—something I was finally ready to tackle. That was when I decided to take a good look at my life, including my past, and discovered who I was and why I made all of the choices I made along the way. I'd never really lived—I just was. I was not awake or aware until I started taking a hard look inside. This self-awareness showed me a lot about myself, which led me to being the happiest I'd ever been by my fiftieth birthday. Letting go of my past mistakes, anger, and guilt freed me to find my peace.

Mike Swift

"Start a movement, not a trend."

COLLEGE ATTENDED: Culinary Institute of America
PROFESSION: Chef in training

I am generally not a jealous person, but after talking to Mike Swift, I will admit that I was a little envious that, at nineteen years old, he already knows what he is going to do with his life—become a chef. It was really cool to interview someone who is taking his education so seriously at such a young age. It was impressive how clear Mike is about his path and what the future holds. I also wanted to interview Mike because he took a slightly different road in his education by choosing to attend a vocational school over a traditional college. After we spoke, it was obvious to me that traditional college would have postponed his career, whereas culinary school will get him to the exact place he is trying to go. If you know your path, no matter your age, by all means, just go for it.

I think the experience Mike gained by going to work in a kitchen for forty hours a week at age thirteen helped him mature earlier than most kids. When

I asked Mike what sets him apart from a regular kid his age who wants to be a chef or go to culinary school, he said that he focused on the big picture by not limiting himself to only thinking about getting a job. Mike also explained his commitment and determination to create a brand instead of owning a single restaurant. It's rare to know someone so young who is already thinking about the big picture.

Although Mike was offered the opportunity to do an externship at two of the fanciest restaurants in New York City, he did something most aspiring young chefs wouldn't have the courage to do—he turned them both down. He made the decision based on what was best for him and knowing where he wants to go in life. The jobs being offered wouldn't help get him to where he wanted to go, and even though they were at big-name restaurants, he knew he had to take a different path. It was refreshing to hear Mike's reasons for turning down the offers. He explained that although he was willing to do the menial tasks required, he knew the experience wouldn't broaden his culinary expertise. He gravitates toward the most hands-on experiences because he feels that is where he gets the best training. How you choose to spend your time matters, so make the best of it and listen to what your gut is telling you.

Mike doesn't have an ounce of regret in choosing culinary school over traditional college. His confidence is contagious and inspiring. It's a blessing to know what you want to do early in life and to be that clear about how to achieve it. Some people take their whole lives and never get there, so having it at such a young age is a real gift.

I started working in restaurants when I was thirteen years old. At first I was mostly doing dishwashing and helping the sous chef prep. It was a job where I could make the most money at such a young age. I didn't expect to fall in love with cooking. It just happened. Working behind the scenes at a restaurant is a different experience than being in the front of the house or a patron. A busy kitchen can be a scary place, but I never strayed from my passion or goal. I was really lucky to have good chef mentors all the way through high school. By the time I graduated, it was obvious to me that a traditional college path wasn't the right choice.

At first, my parents were confused about my decision not to go to college. They kept pushing me to go to community college to see if I would like that, but I knew what I wanted to do. To make my parents happy and to be absolutely certain of my decision, I visited some colleges, including the Culinary Institute of America. When I toured CIA, the students were focused and driven. It wasn't only a couple of kids who appeared that way—everyone I came into contact with was dedicated to their classes and studies. While I wouldn't equate it to military school, it is very rigid, with an emphasis on dedication and discipline. I think it makes the whole college experience better if you are surrounded with like-minded people. After looking at several colleges, I felt culinary school was where I belonged. Everything in my gut told me that I had to pursue my passion and my career to the fullest extent to see how far I could go with it.

I came into culinary school with more experience than a lot of the kids in my class. It wasn't as big a shock for me when our days started off in a lineup where someone made sure our fingernails were properly clipped, and our faces were cleanly shaven. There's a big difference in people from the first day to the last day of school. What I didn't expect was the amount of academic work required at culinary school. It isn't all about cooking. I was expected to write essays like I would in a traditional college, so the educational aspect is very solid for someone attending culinary school.

The associate degree program is eighteen months long. During your summer break, you are required to do an externship. Every few months, CIA offers a career fair where 150 employers come to the school to interview and hire students to work at their restaurants, country clubs, hotels, and other dining establishments. There were a couple of high-end restaurants in New York City that I was interested in working at until I realized the kitchen environment was not what I was looking for. I didn't want to stand at a counter peeling potatoes or carrots for twelve hours a day. They would have to be done in such a precise manner that they didn't appear peeled. No lines, perfectly round, and no skin remaining. Another restaurant said my job would be to pick fifteen hundred cilantro leaves off the stems and count them—every day. It was an honor to be considered, but I didn't feel like it would have done much for me as my first externship. It's not that I felt above it so much as I already had that experience as a prep cook in high school. I was willing to take on any responsibility given to me as long as it was also an opportunity to learn something practical and new. Ultimately, I chose to work at a country club with four different restaurants that I would be allowed to cycle through and see more diverse culinary applications. I think the whole purpose of doing an internship or externship is to gain valuable experiences doing the work that interests you most. It also gives insights into areas you might have been intrigued by but realize aren't right for you. Getting hands-on experience in your prospective career is important.

The biggest thing I am trying to do while working and studying is to build as many connections as possible. I am not as focused on what I will do after graduation because I know I will get a job. Instead, I am accumulating a large cloud of ideas and connections. When I am two or three months away from graduation, I can reach out to people and create my best options and opportunities to launch a business or prospects for jobs. No one taught me to do this. I paid attention when I saw other people operate this way, especially Chef Tony Panza, whom I worked for in high school and who was my first mentor.

Chef Panza allowed me to spend forty hours a week in his kitchen. It was insanity, but I kept going. Whenever someone of influence came into the restaurant, I saw how Chef Panza interacted with his guests. To me, he was the epitome of success, and I wanted to be just like him. I learned even more by paying attention to every detail in the kitchen and the dining room. I was up on my feet doing things that educated me a lot more than being taught practical applications and theories of management in a classroom. Whenever there was a business transaction at the restaurant, I was like a fly on the wall and observed how it went. I always tell people that observation is the best way to voraciously learn any business. As a result, today I am instinctively doing what I saw Tony do for years, and I have no doubt that I can become successful too.

Once I moved on to culinary school, more opportunities arose to learn from experienced teachers and bosses. Every chance that was offered, I took, whether it was a one-day job or a team culinary competition. I have always been an aggressive learner, and that has worked in my favor.

When I look toward my future, I don't want to set limits for myself. One of my goals is to someday open my own restaurant, but more important, I want to create my own brand. If you limit yourself to one restaurant, then you really limit your potential. I have no fear thinking differently from most people coming out of culinary school, and I'm also willing to break barriers doing it. You need creativity in the kitchen, but you also need to think outside the food you prepare, the flavor combinations, different plating styles, and the menu being offered. To set myself apart from the rest of the pack, I need to have more of a movement than a trendy idea.

These days, I feel like I am living the dream. Some of my friends went away to college; others stayed home and got jobs or attended community college. Unfortunately, I've noticed that most of them are stuck doing the same things we were all doing in high school or are studying something they really hate. I am lucky and blessed to be following my passion and doing something I truly enjoy. I don't have the pressure of wondering what is to come because today I am doing what I want and am in control of my future.

Serena Williams

"Things in life don't come easy. You have to work for them."

EDUCATION: University of Massachusetts Amherst and The Art Institute of Fort Lauderdale

OCCUPATION: Professional tennis player

Serena Williams is a perfect example of someone who has been able to make a career out of her passion. While she has been able to become wildly successful as a world champion tennis player, she is also well prepared for her plans after her sports career comes to an end.

I have always admired the fact that Serena is more than a renowned tennis player; she is known around the fashion world and has even created her own line of clothing and accessories. I always love watching someone as talented as Serena play her sport, and I have always admired her drive and ambition. Even though Serena is one of those childhood tennis prodigies, getting an education was always important to her. She earned her GED while touring the world playing tennis and is in pursuit of her college degree. While it may take her a little longer than most to achieve that goal since she is touring the world playing tennis, she has never lost sight of the relevance and significance a good education brings.

Although tennis has been my primary focus since I was fourteen years old, I've made time to pursue my education in both fashion and business. While I was touring, I found time to finish high school and take college courses online. I want to get my degree in business and hope to accomplish that someday. Even though I've had a tremendous career in tennis, getting a college degree has been important to me because I believe it's always smart to have a backup plan. My dad always told me it was important to get an education because anything can happen to an athlete in professional sports, so I'm in pursuit of completing my higher education.

I have always had an interest in fashion, both on and off the tennis court, with my own line of handbags, jewelry, designer wear, and even nail polish. I went to fashion school for a couple of years and even became a certified nail technician before launching my line of nail polish. I've been slowly building several businesses over the years so I will have something to fall back on when I retire from tennis someday.

I think there's a misconception that a college degree alone is enough to get you a job. I don't believe that's true.

You need to put in hard work and be dedicated as well. I learned all about both training to be a champion tennis player. My dedication and love for my career is what I believe truly defines me. It's important to be passionate about what you do. I think a lot of college graduates make a mistake in taking the first job that comes their way when they ought to focus on what career path they really want. My best education has come from my parents and my own trial and error.

Everyone discovers their passion in different ways. It's important to pay attention to things that make you happy. Your quality of life depends on your attitude toward the things that happen to you. It's imperative to keep a positive attitude, even when things aren't going your way. It's also important to stay humble and grateful for what you have instead of focusing on what's missing in your life. To make it in the real world, you have to be ready for hard work, be patient, and be able to handle disappointment. Keep an open mind to learn from your experiences. Things in life don't come easy. You have to work for them. Be grateful and appreciative of each day.

Arnold Schwarzenegger

"It is going to be tough if you look for the easy way out because very rarely is there an easy way out. There is nothing that replaces hard work."

COLLEGES ATTENDED: Santa Monica College, UCLA Extension, and the University of Wisconsin, bachelor's degree in business

OCCUPATION: Actor, producer, businessman, and former governor of California

I have always admired my father's drive and determination when it comes to achieving his dreams. He came to America eager to learn about business and broaden his knowledge about being smart financially. He had a clear vision for himself and knew that while the goals he set for himself seemed out of reach or impossible, he would work relentlessly to get himself there, with failure never being an option. He is a great example of someone who really started out with nothing and has been able to work his way up to achieving great things.

When I was growing up, my dad always spoke to me about the importance of working hard doing what I love and to always be aware of smart ways to invest. He always wanted me to know that there isn't a set age when you should start working; being ahead of the game and not letting anyone stand in your way is the key to success. My dad has never let anyone or anything stand in the way of his dreams. With strength and determination you can do anything you want in life, as long as you believe in yourself, because if you don't, no one else will.

Growing up in Austria, I don't remember making an official transition from attending school to being in the "real world." I didn't grow up where someone actually prepared me for college. In fact, it wasn't even a choice. My friends and I were groomed for learning a skill at trade school in order to become something like a plumber, carpenter, salesman, baker, or mechanic. As early as age fifteen, I made my own money while I studied a trade. It was quite common for kids my age to contribute a little of our monthly income to our family's household expenses. I was in the real world before I even realized what the real world was.

While many kids continued studying their trade in school, I developed other plans. I had a specific goal in mind of what I wanted to do with my life and what kind of career I wanted to have. Therefore, I always felt like I didn't fall into the category of any normal circumstance because I wanted to become a world champion in bodybuilding, weightlifting, or powerlifting. Once I began fully focusing on my goal and creating a vision, I worked hard to educate myself on bodybuilding and improved my strength. I considered these things great investments in my future.

I was inspired by the career Reg Park had made for himself and wanted to take a similar route. Reg not only won the title of Mr. Universe but also went on to star in a series of *Hercules* movies in Hollywood. I figured if I also won the Mr. Universe title a few times, maybe I could get into movies. And if I could get into movies, maybe I could make a lot of money for myself. It all seemed achievable if I completely applied myself and put in the hard work and determination. At a young age, I was convinced that if I followed my plan, I would be successful. As far back as ten years old I was already planning on coming to America; I just wasn't sure how to do it. Many people laughed and said, "Everyone wants to live in America. You are crazy. It will never happen." But I was still inspired because I had a cousin who had moved to America. I knew it was possible for me to do the same.

Fortunately, I had an iron will. While others were out partying, I was training. While they were out dancing at the clubs, I was training . . . and training . . . and training. I also took the time to start studying English because when I moved to America I would need to be able to speak the language. Sure, I could have stayed in Austria and become a police officer like my dad or gone into the army to become an officer, but in my mind, it was my plan or nothing. My sights were set on my goal, and nothing short of that was going to satisfy me.

Although attending college was never a part of my early plans, after relocating to Southern California I soon realized that I needed to improve my English. At that time, Santa Monica College was the place for foreign students to learn the language, so I enrolled in classes. I enjoyed the English classes and ended up adding business marketing, accounting, and math classes as well. Soon I was attending weekly classes, working out in the gym up to five hours a day, and doing construction work to help pay my bills. An acting class was soon added to my routine, and my schedule couldn't have been busier. All of the hard work was essential because it was going to help me carry out my overall plan.

Although I never set out to earn a college degree, almost eight years after taking my first class at Santa Monica College and a few classes at the University of Wisconsin, I was able to pool my credits and earn a diploma from the University of Wisconsin.

By 1978, my film career had taken off. I was cast in a role for *The Jayne Mansfield Story*, played a part in *The Villain* with Kirk Douglas and Ann-Margret, and was well into preparing for my role as *Conan the Barbarian*. My days spent attending classes, working construction, and training in the gym had been replaced with hours of horseback riding and sword fighting. It was an exciting time, and I was finally beginning to realize my dream of not only being a dominant bodybuilding champion and following in the footsteps of Reg Park, but so much more. As a young boy growing up in Austria, I never could have guessed how much success I would be able to achieve through all of my determination.

I maintained the sensibility I had for budgeting my money from a young age and understood how important managing my finances was going to be in securing my future. Instead of spending the money I was making on luxuries, I decided to invest in real estate. When I explained to friends that I was saving to buy a house, they told me to consider putting my money into a rental property where I would be able to use rent coming in to pay off the mortgage instead of taking it from my own pocket. It turned out to be great advice. I quickly realized, as many of my friends already had, that the profits from real estate sales were more than any salary we would have gotten from working a regular job at that time. Over the years, I progressed from buying and selling a 6-unit building to a 12-unit and then a 36-unit building, and then ultimately 100 units. I accomplished this by following a set plan where I rolled the majority of the profits from the previous sale into the next property I had my eyes on. This strategy proved to be incredibly successful and helped maintain my financial security until my movie career really started taking off.

Despite the fact that I had earned a college diploma, I never thought it was something I needed to have to succeed. I craved knowledge and education. I enrolled in individual classes if I believed they were going to aid me in my journey to achieve my dreams. I see far too many people in America chasing after a college diploma simply because it is expected of them. In this country, it is viewed as a minimum requirement everyone should have. In my mind, it is wrong to think that is all you need to succeed. There are too many lost souls out there with college degrees, not knowing where to go next. Many young people today are getting a promise in the beginning that you need to have a college degree, and then no one is sure what to do with it. This degree may serve as a valuable foundation of knowledge, but it is much more important to understand your talents and interests.

I believe everyone has a passion for something, and many times the tendency is to kind of rob you of that passion and push you into what everyone does. That may be beneficial for many kids but not for all of them who go to college. I think a lot of them would be better off learning a trade, something they can use for the rest of their lives.

The biggest mistake I see young people making after earning their college diplomas and leaving school is basically being frozen and waiting for something to happen. It seems like fear sets in as they struggle to decide what they are going to do for the rest of their lives. Young people should not put themselves under that type of pressure. At the same time they are trying to find their way, everyone around them is asking, "What are you going to do?"

First of all, you don't *have* to do anything, but doing something is better than nothing. If you decide to take a job as a cashier at a clothing store to earn some money, you are not going to be locked into that position for the rest of your life unless you want to be. It is a learning experience along your path. When you go and do different things, you will eventually find what you are truly passionate about. You probably aren't going to find it by sitting back and trying to pick what you are interested in without having any experience. You could find your passion one minute or three years after you get out of college. The point is not to sit back. Go out there and do something, anything.

Don't forget that you are not going to "get stuck" where you start out. Many aspiring actors earn four-year college degrees and then move to California to become waiters. They are not just waiting tables in Hollywood restaurants. They are networking and meeting other actors, producers, and directors. It is part of their journey to achieving their goal. The successful actor Harrison Ford was a skilled carpenter before he ever landed his first movie role. His passion was to work with his hands, and then his passion was to have an acting career. Everything seemed to work out pretty well for him in the end.

The most important thing for all of us is not money. It is feeling productive. My father always told me, "*Etwas tun. Nützlich sein.* (Do something. Be useful.)" And over my life I have learned that feeling useful is much more powerful than a big paycheck.

Gayle King

"I didn't graduate college thinking,
All right, life, I am ready. . . ."

COLLEGE ATTENDED: University of Maryland, bachelor's degree in psychology

OCCUPATION: Television anchor, *CBS This Morning*; editor-at-large for *O* magazine

Gayle King is one of those women that you just want to talk to for hours to hear all of the amazing life lessons she has to offer. She has so many great stories about her journey to where she is now—co-anchor of *CBS This Morning* and editor-at-large for *O* magazine. She is smart, approachable, and relatable and has a fantastic sense of humor.

Gayle is a great example of someone who started from the bottom and worked her way up the television ladder of success. She took a traditional route out of college, starting with an entry-level position at a TV station as a production assistant, which led to her getting a job in Baltimore at Channel 13 WJZ, where she met both my mother and Oprah. She continued on this path and worked up the ladder of success to be where she is today at CBS.

One of the other reasons I wanted to interview Gayle for this book is that she could offer a perspective of being a parent, having two children who graduated from college, and dealing with her kids taking a different path than she did. I think being able to get a parent's view on our generation and the difference of what the world is like for us when we graduate compared to how it was for someone like Gayle when she graduated is really interesting. Parents must step back and let their children make their own decisions—which can be challenging, as Gayle mentions in her story—but being a supportive parent no matter what career her children chose has been key to Gayle's success as a mother.

Gayle is one of those women who, like my mom, has been able to juggle it all, and I admire her for that. She has had a successful career as a journalist and has been able to experiment in other jobs, which she also does well, all the while being a hands-on and involved mother. I hope you will enjoy the advice from Gayle as much as I did, and take the advice she offers as both a college graduate and a parent.

$\longleftrightarrow$

I fell in love with journalism during my junior year in college while I was working at a television station as a production assistant. It was an entry-level position that basically entailed me typing up text for the Chyron, the television graphics you used to see over the newscaster's shoulder during a report, and pulling slides to match the text. At the time, I was majoring in psychology. I thought about one day becoming a child psychologist or maybe continuing on to law school, but there was nothing quite like the feeling I got being in the newsroom when breaking news was coming in. From that point on, I knew I was going to do something involved with television.

I didn't come out of college thinking that I was prepared for life. What do you really know about being prepared at such a young age? I was raised to go to college, get a job, and just start working right after graduation so I could support myself. There was no downtime, time-outs, or taking a year off to figure things out. Immediately after graduation, I got a job in Baltimore at Channel 13 WJZ.

After college, I was confronted with many realities of day-to-day life that I hadn't taken time to think about or had previously taken for granted, such as having to buy my own salt and pepper shakers and having to spend half the day in a Laundromat. I also needed to make enough money to get an apartment and make sure there was gas in my car. It was overwhelming, but I still loved the new sense of independence. This was what real life was all about.

When you get out of school, you think you are so grown up and adult. There is still so much you don't know. I look back on my life at twenty-two thinking I was so mature, and the truth is I was still a baby. I had so much growing up left to do and a lot to learn. Not just about myself, but about life and the world and the people I would eventually come into contact with on various jobs while navigating my career. Most people aren't prepared for real life when they leave college, but many of us have been raised to believe that when you graduate, you are a full-blown adult and therefore should be ready for real life. The reality is, you don't even know what you don't know. Experience only comes from doing. Think of it like learning to drive a car. People get their driver's license when they are sixteen and think they are ready for the open road. But so much of becoming a good driver comes with experience: knowing how to navigate the road and defensively looking out for other drivers. You will definitely have a few bumps along the way, but as long as they aren't life-altering, those are the experiences that teach us to be better drivers. The same idea holds true when it comes to figuring out what you want to do in your life.

Although you don't need to have the exact answer when you graduate, I think you ought to have some idea of what you want to do when you get out of school so you can get out there and try it. This is especially true if you have bills to pay or are mired down with college loan debt.

College loan debt has become a trillion-dollar problem for kids coming out of school, most of whom wonder why they paid so much money to accumulate such a large debt. While a college degree is important for your sense of responsibility, it also teaches you commitment and how to get along with others.

Understand and accept that you won't love every job you have over the years, and you're not supposed to. You are going to go through times where you don't like the people you work with, the atmosphere or office environment, or even your boss. That's okay, as long as you get something out of the experience. Every opportunity leads to something else. Unfortunately, these days I have noticed a certain attitude from young graduates who believe that they don't need to stay in a job if they don't like it. I don't think that's the right approach. Job-hopping doesn't look good to potential employers. I come from a generation that believes if you make a commitment, you need to keep it.

When my son, Will, graduated from Duke, he took a job in investment banking in New York. He had interned with a boutique firm when he was in college, so he was offered the job before he graduated. He majored in Chinese and wasn't the least bit interested in the job—and it showed—but for security, he took it anyway. He wanted to quit with no other job lined up. I freaked out because I grew up believing you don't quit a job unless you've got another one to go to. I thought he should stick it out at the investment banking firm while he looked for another job to go to. I did my best to explain that it was far better to get a new job as an employed person. My son didn't see it that way. He explained how unhappy he was in his current position, and then I realized that it was affecting his health. He wasn't sleeping, he was a constant nervous wreck, and he was losing a lot of weight. I am all for working hard but not so hard that it endangers your health. Although I didn't agree with his decision to leave his position without having someplace else to go, as a parent, I didn't want to see my son suffer, so I had to back off and let him make his own choices. When I did, he assured me he would find something else and everything would be fine. In the end, I wanted him to know that I supported him in whatever he decided to do.

Instead of allowing my disapproval to hold him back, my son took measures to move toward the thing he really wanted to do—build an Internet startup in China. Without a job, he moved to Shanghai, where he soon discovered that a top video gaming company was opening an office. My son is now working in a job that he is passionate about, running their office in China. Best of all, he is happy, thriving, and doing something he loves.

My daughter, Kirby, graduated from college and went on to get her master's degree in public health at Columbia University. Shortly after she graduated from Columbia, she was offered a job with the Robin Hood Foundation, a charitable organization founded by the successful hedge fund manager Paul Tudor Jones to alleviate problems caused by poverty in New York City. Kirby has since moved to Washington, D.C., where she works at the Department of Health. I know how hard it can be for kids to get jobs right out of school and recognize that my kids were fortunate to both land jobs straight out of college that led them to careers they find both rewarding and fulfilling.

At the end of the day, nothing beats experience: putting yourself out there in an entry-level position and learning everything you can about the job you think you want. Find someone you think is good at doing what you want to do and figure out a way to work for that person.

Even in a down economy, the road to success hasn't changed over the years. Everyone notices people who are good at what they do and who love their work. Companies always notice someone who is a go-getter, who is willing to speak up with a good idea, and who stands out from the crowd by going above and beyond the call of duty. The people who don't mind working hard, putting in long hours, and giving up their weekends are the people who rise to the top. Don't just "be" at your job, be *interested in* your job. Engage in the work and opportunities in front of you instead of showing up, punching the clock, and looking at your watch trying to figure out how much longer you have to be there before going home.

Love what you do and let your customers, co-workers, and boss see your commitment, passion, and enjoyment. To me, that's the true meaning of success.

Candace Nelson

*"You don't become an entrepreneur if
you don't appreciate a challenge. You have
to be willing to sacrifice."*

COLLEGE ATTENDED: Wesleyan University, bachelor's degree in economics

OCCUPATION: Founder, Sprinkles Cupcakes

I was in high school when Sprinkles Cupcakes opened
its first location in Beverly Hills, California. It was an
instant hit and became an obsession for everyone I
know. I can't recall driving by Sprinkles without seeing
a long line of people waiting outside the door. Not only
did it become the new hot spot for all of my friends to
get a sweet treat, but it also became a tourist attraction.
I loved interviewing Candace because I enjoyed hearing how someone went from a traditional path right
out of college, first working in investment banking and
then working for a dot-com company, to following her
true passion by enrolling in pastry school when the dot-
com industry crashed. It's hard for people my age to
understand that the Internet was something new back
in the 1990s. While we've grown up taking the Internet

for granted, people like Candace were pioneering the industry. Companies came and went fast, wiping out jobs and eventually the local economy in the Bay Area. It was life altering for those who were a part of the dot-com bust, many of whom thought they were in stable jobs but ended up broke and having to start over.

Candace approached her challenge as an opportunity, making the most out of a potentially disastrous situation. I love the way she phrased that time in her life because it is so relevant for almost any situation we might face, but especially now, when you may be trying to figure out what you are going to do next. Candace went back to her roots, doing what she found fun and what brought her joy.

As someone who is interested in baking, I think it is inspiring to see how Candace's idea has gone on to inspire so many other women to create their own bakeries and follow their dreams. The cupcake fad became huge, turning a common baked good into something more than just food. It became an industry. Candace is a great role model for our generation because she represents someone who took a risk to try something that had never been done before—something I think a lot of people are tempted to do. Candace's business is much more than baking cupcakes. Today you can't go to any website or gift store without seeing something cupcake themed. Without her innovation, I am not sure this would be the case.

Listening to Candace talk about the importance of paying your dues, putting in the hard work to get what you want, and remaining open to all possibilities is great advice. I know firsthand there are no shortcuts to making it. People sometimes think you can circumvent the process, but you can't. It was cool to hear Candace admit that she experienced self-doubt almost every day while she was building her company. But she was also willing to sacrifice a lot in order to get what she wanted. You can't always have it all, but Candace is a great example of how you can have fun while creating a job that doesn't exist and doing everything it takes to make it a huge success.

I chose to go to a liberal arts college because I thought it would help me become a well-rounded, educated person. I thought studying economics would give me a good basis for working in the business world. By the time I got to my senior year, I had a pretty good idea of what I wanted to do when I graduated. A decent number of people from my class were going to work at investment banks. I had heard that was a good first exposure to working with companies in an intense way and would open up a lot of opportunities, so I gravitated toward that as my career.

I began applying for jobs in my senior year and interviewing with different financial firms all over the country, and I was recruited into an analyst program with an investment banking firm. Being an analyst is an incredibly grueling position that requires long hours and being super organized and on time to meet deadlines. Even though I was offered the job, I was nervous about taking it because I didn't know if I could succeed. I was worried about all of the stories I'd heard about how challenging the investment analyst positions are and I wasn't sure if it was something I was passionate about doing.

All sorts of doubt flooded my mind. I didn't have the option of moving back home or taking time off after graduating. I needed to support myself out of the gate, and it was a logical and pragmatic decision for me. That awakening was a real shock from my lackadaisical lifestyle in college. In the two-year program in corporate finance, I worked with high-tech companies in San Francisco and IPOs, mergers, and acquisitions. I remained in the program for the full two years. Although I was offered an extension to stay, I opted not to. It was the height of the first dot-com explosion, and the thing to do at the time was go to work for an Internet company. Instead of taking a third year, I went to work for an Internet company in business development for the next couple of years.

I was young and making decisions about my future that felt dramatic because the dot-com boom led to the subsequent dot-com bust. San Francisco and the entire Bay Area encountered a recession that was a precursor to the one the nation just went through. Everything that had been on my résumé, from investment banking to working for a dot-com, meant nothing. My career vanished overnight. And so did many of my friends and peers, as there was a mass exodus out of the Bay Area. There were no jobs, and the economy was in the absolute doldrums. I wasn't ready to leave yet. By this time, I had met and married my husband, who also worked in investment banking, and we weren't sure where we wanted to go. So I used this challenge as an opportunity to test whether my passion for baking could be a career. I had already lived one extreme, doing something I was not passionate about and devoting twenty hours a day to it. I knew I didn't want to do that anymore. I decided to listen to the old adage "Do what you are passionate about." I opted to go to pastry school while all of my friends were going to business school. I enrolled at Tante Marie's professional pastry program in San Francisco.

Baking was always an important part of my family life. I baked with my mom and my great-grandmother, who was well known in San Francisco in the 1930s for her restaurants and desserts. I grew up hearing about her legendary baked goods. My first recollection of being drawn to baking was when I was a young girl living with my family in Indonesia. I had a hankering for a chocolate chip cookie, something you couldn't easily find in a bakery where I was, so I had to make it. American desserts were my connection to home. I always thought of baking as something you did as a hobby, not as a way to make a living.

I remember the first time I discovered Mrs. Fields. I was in first grade when I visited the store. The cookies were expensive, and I thought it was fascinating that they weighed them to see how much they cost. It felt exotic and exciting. Aside from my great-grandmother, Mrs. Fields was my first female role model. She was an inspiration because at the time, no other woman had made it in the baking industry.

When I decided to enroll in pastry school, some people warned me that your hobby stops being joyful when you start doing it every day. But I figured that at the end of the day, I would know how to make beautiful desserts even if I decided not to make a living doing it. If I decided not to pursue baking as my next career, it wouldn't be the end of the world; I was still young and educated and would be able to get another job. Luckily, I didn't have to face that option because I fell in love with baking and started looking at it from a whole new perspective.

A lot of people go to pastry school hoping to get a job working in a restaurant, on a cruise ship, or at a hotel and make a career out of it. I assessed the market and saw a business opportunity. I realized there were various needs in the marketplace, and I thought I could fill those needs in a new and creative way. I thought I had a contribution to make, though I wasn't exactly sure what it was. My idea to start a business in baking came about through working and creating while being open to the possibilities of different options.

When I graduated from pastry school, I started by creating a dessert catering business. I wanted to make artful desserts for special occasions. I was intrigued with cake decorating and thought this kind of approach would tap my creativity. My husband was incredibly supportive of my endeavor. Here was a man with his MBA, holding my triple-tier cakes in his lap while I drove up and down the steep hills of San Francisco delivering them to customers. I realized that special-occasion cakes are really just that— for special occasions—which meant that people don't buy them that often. I wanted to create something people could enjoy on a daily basis or at the very least, frequently. That's when it occurred to me that a cupcake, made in an artful way, using ingredients of the special-occasion cake, was a new and fresh take on desserts. That was the essence of Sprinkles.

Getting this idea off the ground sounds logical today, but at the time, it was such a novel idea that it was challenging to pursue. Cupcakes were usually found in the supermarket, made with shortening and really gross frosting. They typically weren't made fresh or with high-quality ingredients. I had a more sophisticated take on the classic cupcake and decided to use the finest ingredients, such as sweet cream butter, pure Nielsen-Massey Madagascar Bourbon vanilla, and Callebaut chocolate. When I started baking cupcakes my way, I created a niche that people responded to. That was my first indication that I might be on to something. I even started experimenting with offbeat offerings such as vegan and gluten-free cupcakes and even dog-food cupcakes for our furry friends.

There are lots of great business ideas, but if they don't resonate with you personally, it is easy not to implement them. That wasn't an option for me. Sprinkles was the first cupcake-only bakery. It was fun to build the business and launch our first store in Beverly Hills in 2005. It was a six-hundred-square-foot space. We sold two thousand cupcakes our first week in business. We now have ten locations around the United States with plans to open in fifteen more cities around the world. To keep things innovative, we also started selling cupcakes out of our "Sprinklesmobile" and developed a "cupcake ATM," so anyone can fulfill their cravings for one of our cupcakes 24/7. We've even developed our own brand of ice cream. We love crazy ideas and aren't afraid to experiment. We are always trying to challenge ourselves to think of the next one.

You don't become an entrepreneur if you don't appreciate a challenge. You have to be willing to sacrifice. Back when I first started baking, while my friends were going on vacations and settling into secure working lives, I threw all of that out the window and put every waking moment into building my business. There was no such thing as taking a vacation. My husband and I missed good friends' weddings, family events, and other milestones to make sure we left no stone unturned. If you want something and it is important to you, you will have to make unimaginable sacrifices to get it.

Ron Bergum

"Once you graduate from college, financial independence is your obligation."

COLLEGE ATTENDED: San Diego State University, bachelor's degree in real estate financial services
OCCUPATION: CEO, Prospect Mortgage

While I was in my junior year of college, I went to see an accountant for the first time in order to gain a better understanding of my finances. I had an allowance in college, which allowed me to understand how much I had to spend on food, clothing, and other things my parents no longer paid for—including my cell phone. It is important to be smart about money and to learn how to manage your finances. I never grew up believing I wouldn't have to work to support myself. I grew up in an area of Los Angeles where the notion of not working because your family has money is common. I was in elementary school the first time I asked my mom about money.

"Your dad and I have money, but you don't," she said.

I'd never forgotten my mom's answer that day because she made it quite clear that while we lived very comfortably, I would have to learn to create that life on my own without the financial help of my parents. Both of my parents instilled a strong work ethic in me from a very young age. They inspired me to earn my own money from the time I was old enough to hold a broom. In fact, most Saturday mornings, my dad got his hair cut at a salon, and my sister and friend and I swept the floors to make some money. I took great pride in doing a good job every weekend and experienced an even greater feeling when it came time for us to collect our money.

When I was in high school and had my first job where taxes were taken out of my paycheck, I was shocked. I was expecting the check to be a little over ninety dollars, and it was actually for forty-eight dollars. I wanted to understand where the missing money went, so I talked to my parents, who explained the various deductions and why they're important. The jolt of that experience made me appreciate the value of a dollar, especially when it came time to buying things I wanted or going to dinner with my friends. I had made some money in college, where I was responsible for paying the taxes, and I wanted to understand how much I could save now and how much I would need to set aside in the future, so I made an appointment with an accountant. I wanted to know that by the time I graduated college, I would have enough money saved to pay my own way.

Once I learned about finances, I became the messenger to my friends to help them understand that they'd better be prepared, because every decision they make today will impact how they live tomorrow. Rent, food, car payments, health insurance, auto insurance, renter's insurance, gym memberships, dining out, movies, cell phone bills, electricity, cable, clothing, and so on are just some of the expenses that become very real after college. And if you have college loan debt, it will follow you until it is paid in full.

I decided to interview Ron Bergum, CEO of Prospect Mortgage, the largest private non-bank-owned mortgage lender in the country, about the importance of financial awareness coming out of college, especially if you have any desire to someday buy a home. For most people, buying a home is the single largest expenditure we will make in our lives. If you aren't careful, that dream may never become a reality. I found Ron's advice enlightening and direct. It's an important topic that no one wants to talk about but needs to hear.

The biggest mistake people make coming out of college is not having an understanding of how to use credit properly. There is an overwhelming tendency to go into debt right away. When you graduate, credit card companies offer you their cards with a certain line of credit. Most kids view that offer as someone giving them free money. If the credit limit is five thousand dollars, most people don't spend that amount on things that are critical for survival. The reality is that you shouldn't go into debt to buy nonessentials, such as clothes, pizza, and vacations. You have to pay that money back with interest if you don't pay the balance in full every month. If you max out your card and are making only the minimum payment each month, because of steep finance charges on most credit cards, a twenty-dollar pizza over time can end up costing you hundreds of dollars! There's no pizza I can think of that is worth that kind of money over time.

If you are working, you have to buy things based on whatever your level of income is. It needs to be in relation to the amount of money you have coming in that isn't already allocated toward rent, car payment, insurance, groceries, utilities, and student loan payments, if you have them. A credit card is a convenience and should be used the same way you would cash. Once you spend cash, it's gone. You don't finance a cash purchase and you don't get to wait thirty days or more to make the payment. You hand over your hard-earned dollars and the transaction is complete. Spending cash doesn't incur debt. It may leave you cash poor, but you won't go into the hole owing more money than you have in the bank ever. The introduction of the debit card helped this philosophy, but it also created another stream of revenue for banks. When your debit account becomes overdrawn, you go into the negative and owe money to the bank for transaction and overdraft fees, which can really add up. You have to be careful about knowing how much money is in the account tied to your debit card or you will find yourself losing money on purchases when you overspend. So what should credit be used for? Credit should only be used in cases where it is a necessity or when it is an emergency. Unless you can pay your balance off at the end of every month, you cannot afford whatever you are purchasing on credit.

You need to have a philosophy of spending and a budget in mind that allows you to never incur debt for non-essentials. Setting a budget is very important. Whether you are in school, out of school, working, or any combination of these, you need to understand how much money you spend every month. You should never carry consumer debt unless it is for the purchase of a car or home.

I strongly suggest living below your means and starting a savings account as soon as possible. Having at least six to twelve months of living expenses in savings is ideal. This number is the same no matter how big your expenses become over time. That money is your safety net, and if you carry that idea through your whole life, you will never have to worry about dealing with the unexpected, unforeseen circumstances that can and often do happen. Some people call this a "rainy day fund," but I call it a *blunt force shock fund* because you never want to dip into your savings. The shock is usually brought on by some unexpected catastrophic event. If you were to suddenly lose your job, you would have enough money to pay your rent, mortgage, car payment, and all of the other critical payments you are obligated to make without the added stress of having no funds to pull from. This is another critical reason to avoid carrying credit card debt. When you don't have enough money to pay for your essentials, the decisions you make at that time aren't going to be the right ones because you will be making them out of panic and desperation. This is never a good combination for making financial decisions.

Most people default on their mortgage loans because they have no shock fund. If they don't have the reserves, they don't have the ability to make their house payment and quickly find themselves in a terrible game of catch-up. Look at your shock fund as something you can't touch unless the worst-case scenario happens. And, by all means, don't use this reserve account for anything else. Don't spend it on a vacation, buy yourself a fancy watch, or over-indulge in clothes or shoes you can't afford. The only time you can start investing is when you have money over and above that reserve.

The first goal is to get to your necessary reserve.

The second goal is to have enough extra money over your reserve to start investing.

Then and only then can you begin budgeting what you want to do with that money, whether it's going on a vacation or buying your first house.

Will the job you are going to get provide you with enough money to cover your daily living expenses and your monthly student loan payment? If the answer is no, you cannot afford to take that job. And if you do, you will likely need to get a second job to cover the rest of your expenses because you do not want to make the mistake of not paying off your student loans in a timely manner.

If you ever dream of someday owning a home, pay your student loans and don't carry consumer debt.

Once you graduate from college, financial independence is your obligation. You start by getting a job and making your own money. Kids should assume that their parents aren't going to keep paying their expenses after they graduate. As soon as you get a job, you will more than likely be off their payroll. It is a view of responsibility that you need to take on to strike your independence. When I graduated from college, I had a job but not enough money saved to buy three suits I could wear to work. I borrowed the money from my parents, but I had to pay it back as soon as I could. I never went back to the well after that. As soon as I got my first paycheck, I gave my parents the money, paid my rent, and put the rest in my reserve fund. That was the protocol I developed as a kid that I took with me throughout my life.

The real world is difficult and full of challenges. People suck sometimes. People aren't always nice. Bad things happen. Companies go out of business. People get fired. You come to work late, and your boss gets pissed off. That stuff happens every day. The only way you learn to get better and learn about what you want to do is by experiencing all of that. Financially, you have to feel that pressure to be supporting yourself because it teaches responsibility and stability for your future.

Ben Kaufman

"Failure is everywhere. Understanding why things succeed and fail is the best sort of learning you can do. If you're not trying new things, you can't fail."

COLLEGE ATTENDED: Champlain College
OCCUPATION: Founder, Mophie and Quirky

I wanted to interview Ben Kaufman because I have been a longtime admirer and user of his Mophie products. I thought it would be beneficial to talk to someone close to my age who had broken out of the traditional path and carved his own way by doing things in a fresh and new style. I also thought it would be interesting to talk to someone whose product is an everyday part of my life and the lives of so many people my age. I use his Mophie juice pack all the time, to the point that I've become reliant on it, especially when I travel and don't have the ability to plug in my phone to recharge the battery when I need to. It's been a lifesaver more than once!

Ben is a renegade for having the courage to take a chance on his invention and follow his instincts while still only in high school. I think it's amazing to see someone so young have an idea and follow through on it. Speaking to Ben was informative for me because he was the first interview I did with someone who started his first company in high school and has maintained his success over the years with multiple companies. I found his take on the real world fascinating, especially as a young entrepreneur who is close in age to you and me. I loved his point of view on asking everyone you can about your idea, invention, or plan to get as much feedback as possible. I feel that this kind of data gathering works especially well for a technology-driven product. When I interviewed Sara Blakely, the inventor of Spanx, her take on other people's opinions was the complete opposite. She believes that other people's opinions can ruin your idea and frustrate you to the point of becoming so discouraged that you lose confidence and don't follow through on it. I found the dichotomy in opinions by two very successful inventors interesting and a little confusing. I suppose the value of getting other people's opinions depends on what your product is, whether you have something new and innovative in technology or you are filling a niche need in the marketplace.

Ben's approach to entering the real world was some of the most straightforward, no-nonsense advice I've heard. Sometimes people want to give you information in small doses so it's easier to digest. They butter you up about reality without giving it to you the way it really is. I appreciated Ben's style. His advice was candid and frank, traits I truly respect. Ben is a tremendous example of someone who wasn't afraid to hustle his product because he knew that in order for it to work, he'd have to believe in it more than anyone else.

Many people view our generation as entitled, spoiled, and arrogant. People could have viewed Ben that way, but they didn't. I gained a lot of insight from Ben as I listened to him talk about people graduating and thinking they know everything. It's important to stay open-minded and current, but also to realize that finishing college isn't the end of education—it's really just the start.

←——————————————————————————→

When I started my first company in high school, I persuaded my parents to remortgage their house to help with the funding. When they said they would, they made me promise that I would go to college. I had an idea for lanyard headphones, which I went on to pursue during my senior year of high school. It was born from a personal need to make using my iPod shuffle easier. It started with a simple idea—and not even a very good one. Even so, these headphones were known as the Song Sling and became the initial product of my first company, Mophie, named after my two golden retrievers, Molly and Sophie. I went to China shortly after the second mortgage came through and stayed for several weeks. I needed to figure out how to find a factory that could make the headphones as I saw them. I flew home and barely graduated from high school.

Ironically, the same day I graduated, Mophie officially launched. I spent the summer driving around the country trying to sell the Song Sling, circling the United States several times hustling.

As promised, I enrolled at Champlain College in Burlington, Vermont, to hold up my end of the bargain with my parents. I suppose I look at that decision as more bribery than desire to go. Mophie was just starting to take off, so I was busy juggling classes while trying to run a startup. I was in class one day when my phone rang. My professor told me if I answered the call, I'd be asked to leave the class. It was my factory in China calling with a problem that needed my immediate attention. For as long as I could remember, learning in the real world was the most important kind of education to me. There I was, in a real-world predicament where I could learn the exact thing I was being taught out of a book, and I was being told I wasn't allowed to do it. I knew that college wasn't where I should be.

In January 2006, I took another product to Macworld, the ultimate three-day fan event for new and upcoming products for Apple devices. Fortunately, a modular case accessory system I created for the iPod nano ended up winning Best in Show that year. The award solidified my decision to leave college and pursue my career as an inventor. My parents weren't completely supportive of my decision, but they understood my position. By this time, it was pretty clear that Mophie was going to be around for a few years. We had enough cash to be in the game for a while.

Their philosophy was, "If this fails in a year or two, we can still force you back to college." Even so, they allowed me the opportunity to explore my alternative path.

I want to be perfectly clear about one thing. I would not advise most people to follow my path and drop out of school just because it worked for me. The traditional path is right for most people, and that is why most people follow it. But an alternative path also works for some people—sometimes better. It's a case-by-case, opportunity-by-opportunity, idea-by-idea decision.

When I dropped out of college, I didn't move back home to live with my parents. I lived in my office in Burlington. I liked it there and I was building my team, so it made sense to stay. To me, it was better than living at home. Besides, everything I was doing back then was more of an experiment. When you experiment, you start with a hypothesis and then you have to work toward a conclusion. I am all about getting to conclusions. So when I decided to live in the office instead of moving back home, I asked myself, "Can I do this? Can I live in the office and still be a happy person?" There is beauty in experiments if you know how to find it. Too many people don't get to that conclusion in the first couple of tests. They hear the word *no* a few times and view that as the conclusion when it's really just a data point. Every week, I work on products and ideas that don't pan out. I have employees that don't work out. I have retailers that don't work out. Failure is everywhere. Understanding why things succeed and fail is the best sort of learning you can do. If you're not trying new things, you can't fail. Be willing to experiment and, by default, willing to fail.

I imagine my life would have been a lot different if I had stayed in college. I couldn't have done what I did or what I am doing if I had spent four years reading about international business and not navigating it. I imagine I would be brainwashed to the point of not taking the risks that I have in the past. When people ask me for advice about trying to create something that interests them, I usually tell them to look at the bottom of their shoe, because Nike said it best: "Just do it!" There really is nothing else to say to people. As soon as you start giving someone advice to the contrary, it may or may not be applicable. You have to try—and when you fail, try again until you find a way to see whatever it is you're aiming for to a point of conclusion. That might come a week after you build your first prototype and you show your friends who all think it sucks, or it may come in a couple of years. Most of the time, you will get to a point of closure where you know whether your idea is good within a few weeks. Get as many opinions as possible. You need to be a strong enough person to know that people are going to give you the truth and sometimes the truth isn't what you want to hear. If you don't hear it before you start, you can count on hearing it after you have already committed and spent half your life or all of your savings doing it. I realize that having people shoot down your idea may be demoralizing, but sometimes it can be empowering, especially when you can prove that you are right, and they are wrong. If you are going to try to make it on the streets, you are going to need to toughen up. Remember, opinions are not conclusive. I was always respectful that I might get to a conclusive place, and in that conclusion, someone might be right that my idea sucked—or they might be wrong. I was always more driven to get to a conclusive place than to try to debate who was right.

What I look for in my employees is that they learned what they needed to from college. If they have a degree in business or design, they can deliver the basic principles that may one day make them good at these things. College gives you the ingredients, but you don't graduate knowing the recipe. I don't always hire people just because they have a college degree—but you'd better have a really great dropout story if you want to work for me. The key to succeeding in the workplace today is realizing you don't know it all, but you can take what you have learned in your life so far and turn it into something useful for yourself, your company, or your product.

Joe Kakaty

"The most significant mistake parents and students make when taking out college loans is borrowing more than they can afford to repay."

COLLEGE ATTENDED: State University of New York, Brockport
OCCUPATION: CEO, EdVisors.com

According to *USA Today*, there is more than $1 trillion of outstanding student loan debt. Looking for a job in the economy today can be a challenging and intimidating process. With so many people graduating from college and trying to find a way to pay off their student loans, the fact that the economy is in such a dark place makes the process that much more challenging. Because of the state of our economy, I thought that it would be important to include someone who could speak to those dealing with student loan debt and explain how to make the process more understandable.

Joe Kakaty is the CEO of a company that works with students to make smarter financial decisions when it comes to paying for an education. I was shocked by everything Joe had to say about student loans and the effects they can have on your life. As tuition increases every year, people planning to get an education need to be more aware of the options they have for education and how to pay for it.

Taking out loans for college isn't something you can just stop dealing with when you graduate. The loans you took out can haunt you for the rest of your life if you don't pay them off on time. Many people rack up such high student debt that it prevents them from taking out future loans or even purchasing a home. It is vital to be aware of the importance of paying your student loans as you go through college and beyond, so that something you did when you were eighteen doesn't continue to chase you throughout your life.

⟵――――――――――――――――――――――――――⟶

The most significant mistake parents and students make when taking out college loans is borrowing more than they can afford to repay. Students who make this mistake are forced to adopt an austere lifestyle, work a second job, use alternative repayment plans such as extended repayment and income-based repayment (if available), or move back in with their parents to save on rent, and this level of discipline is hard to implement if it's not how you have lived your life.

If you're reading this section of the book, you most likely owe money on your student loans. Borrowers who drop out of college often assume that they don't have to repay the debt. But the debt is still owed even if you are dissatisfied with the quality of the education, and even if you don't find a job!

Borrowers who encounter financial difficulty should always talk to their lender before they (even get close to) default. You lose options if you default first, and the debt becomes more expensive. Ignoring the debt does not make it go away. These loans are almost impossible to discharge in bankruptcy. The federal government can garnish wages and social security benefit payments, intercept federal and state income tax refunds, and prevent renewal of a professional license without a court order. Unfortunately, borrowers who are in trouble not only don't call their lenders, but often ignore the mail and telephone calls to their financial peril! Don't be this person. Face your situation and deal with it so you aren't penalized for life.

I also often hear from borrowers who think that being a little late with a payment should not be a problem. But it is. Even if you are only one day late! That's all it takes to ruin a good credit score. Do it often enough and you will become a subprime borrower. Borrowers who want to refinance their loans at a lower rate must make all of the payments on all their debts (not just student loans) on time as per the agreement, within the terms of the promissory note they signed.

Other common errors include extended periods of nonpayment through forbearance, in-school deferment or delinquency, failing to sign up for auto-debit to ensure on-time payment and get a slight discount on the interest rate, failing to claim the student loan interest deduction, and unemployed or underemployed college graduates returning to school to get additional credentials (and subsequently piling on more debt) and blaming the lender instead of taking personal responsibility for their own actions.

The first step to ensure that you don't fall behind on repaying your student loans is to budget for your payments. Create a list of your actual expenses. Track and categorize all of your spending for one month. Borrowers who are struggling to repay their student loans often have difficulty in other areas of their personal finances too. They may have high credit card debt and a high mortgage or auto loan payment. Even professionals such as lawyers and doctors often live paycheck to paycheck. With a budget, they get receipts for every purchase and record the expenses in a spreadsheet or a program such as Quicken or Microsoft Money.

Every expense needs to be categorized as a need or a want (mandatory vs. discretionary) and in broad categories such as food, clothing, shelter, medical care, insurance, taxes, and loan payments. Be realistic: vacation or spring break, a cell phone, and cable TV are luxuries, not necessities. At the end of the month, total all the categories to see what your real expenses add up to. If your expenses exceed your income, you have a difficult situation. Even seemingly mandatory expenses can be cut, such as by moving in with your parents or getting a roommate to save on rent, using public transportation instead of owning a car, and eliminating dining out and entertainment expenses. These short-term sacrifices will pay off later in life.

Just being aware of spending patterns will help you exercise restraint. This extreme discipline will be rewarded many times over because it will help teach you financial responsibility that lasts a lifetime.

Dr. Dan Siegel

WHEN MOVING HOME MEETS MIXED EMOTIONS

"When you are back to the physical location of 'home,' it is easy to fall back into that old identity as the child of your parents."

COLLEGE ATTENDED: UCLA

This chapter is intended to help you understand all of the internal conflict you may experience after college, especially if, like me, you choose to move home for some period of time. This is also a great section for your parents to read to help them understand the way you're feeling and how they may be feeling too.

Even though I love spending time with my family and being around them 24/7, it was genuinely frustrating for me to be living back home after graduating because it didn't feel like I was propelling myself in a forward direction. In fact, I feared it would inhibit my progress into adulthood—that my life would feel like I was back in high school again. There would be rules, people wanting to know where I was going and when I would be back. I would have to realize that it wasn't all about me anymore because there were going to be four other people living in the house as well. A huge part of me knew that I wanted to be independent, come and go as I pleased, make my own money, and perhaps save a little while living at home. Even though my mom didn't ask me to pay rent, I also didn't want her to pay for my extras. I was capable of making my own money and fortunately had saved some from the work I'd done while I was in school. So I decided to tell my mom that I would be financially responsible for the things I buy and do. In my mind, this was the only way I could be okay with moving back home. When I made the decision, my mom supported me but always managed to stay neutral.

These days, millions of kids are moving back in with their families after school. A recent study showed that nearly 40 percent of people under age thirty-one are living at home with their parents. I know that many of you reading this will relate to how I felt, as I am sure you are probably similarly dealing with an overload of conflicting emotions. And while this period of time can be extremely challenging for us college graduates, it is also a confusing and challenging time for our parents. For parents, dealing with a child's roller coaster of emotions can be difficult to understand and can often cause conflict. But it doesn't have to be that way.

I thought it might be helpful to give you some insight about what your struggles after graduation really mean. I reached out to Dr. Dan Siegel, a clinical professor of psychiatry at the UCLA School of Medicine, to ask him to help explain some of the emotions you may feel as you face graduation and the months to come.

When you're away at college, you have a period of independence. For the most part, you were living on your own, making your own decisions, with no one looking over your shoulder or telling you what time to come home. Dr. Siegel's insights helped me understand that our brain has a chemical response when we find ourselves living at home after college. Dealing with the flood of various emotions and not knowing exactly how you feel is hard. His concept of the old feelings rearing their head makes complete sense and gave meaning to why I felt so ambivalent. So if you are feeling stuck, awkward, angry, or confused while you're living at home, know that it's mostly old feelings coming up for you and totally normal. Don't allow your feelings to hold you back or make your experience miserable. Understand it, accept it, and keep moving toward your goals.

We've grown up in an era with a lot of emphasis placed on outward interactions instead of being inwardly focused. We tweet, post on Facebook, upload pictures to Instagram, and check in on Foursquare so people we know—or don't know—can follow our every move, milestone, accomplishment, and meal. What's happened as a result of this external focus is that many of you may have lost or never developed the ability to look inward and reflect for a moment and listen to what your heart is telling you.

Checking in with your heart and gut is important.

The term *heartfelt sense* is not just a poet's metaphor. I was curious about offering some advice to help you look inward and to have a deep understanding of what you feel.

Being able to discuss all of my experiences with Dr. Siegel was eye-opening and made me feel a lot better about the way I felt when I first moved home after college. When I met with Dr. Siegel for this book, he had me do a series of exercises in which he asked me to play the role of both parent and child so I could see both points of view. I hadn't thought of what it might feel like from my parents' point of view before. Dr. Siegel helped me understand that keeping an open dialogue between parents and children is the most useful and effective way for all parties to deal with the transition. So keep in mind that although this time may be frustrating for you, it can be just as challenging for your parents too.

⟵————————————————————⟶

When you suddenly find yourself done with college and living at home again, your identity that is "you living with your parents" gets reactivated, when you have spent all of this time developing an identity of "you independent from your parents." Right away, there is potential conflict because people are incredibly settled in a strong identity when they are away from their parents, but when they come back to live with their parents, it evokes the old ways of being. You get lost in familiar places. There will be an automatic challenge that you should expect. The old "child" identity of the older adolescent returns. Since you haven't established your own family, job, or place in society, when you come back to the physical location of "home," it is easy to fall back into that old identity as the child of your parents. For the first time in your life, you are living without structure. For a lot of people, that can be terrifying. Three really big uncomfortable emotions bubble up: fear, sadness, and anger. Each can come out in the form of conflict, inner and outward. These feelings can be incredibly confusing, but there are ways to tackle the situation before things implode.

If your parents have a meeting with you that lays out the understanding of why you've moved back home, whether for economic reasons or just to give you time to get on your feet, there will be less conflict. If you're a parent reading this, sit down with your kids and say something like, "I respect who you are as a person. I respect everything you have been through these last four years and your decision to move back into our home for now. But we have to work out the rules." And then express your expectations in a calm, rational, and clear way. Make sure you let each other know what the standards are up front. What are you willing to accept and live up to during this time period?

For example, my wife and I have a certain standard of cleanliness we live in. Our son had been living with some friends throughout college, and their level of acceptable cleanliness didn't match ours. When my son moved back home to live with us, I made it clear that he would have to raise his standards because we weren't about to drop ours. After that, we never had an issue again. Clear and thought-out communication is important in every relationship, but it's especially important when you are dealing with an older adolescent trying to find his or her own way.

Parents, remember that your child wants to feel seen, safe, and soothed. Yelling at your child to get off the couch and get a job isn't the best approach to motivating him or her to begin the next phase of his or her life. The benefits of helping your child get a job are not strictly financial. The money is important, but the crucial thing is that your child feels a sense of accomplishment. A job may not be considered "fun," but your child must be able to find the art of being present in whatever he or she is doing.

If you want to be effective in guiding your child toward this approach, let him or her know you understand that it is really important to feel accomplished—to get a result and feel rewarded for one's efforts. It isn't important what your child does as long as he or she has a deep sense of satisfaction. I always advise parents that the key thing for your child to know is how to be present in life. One of the best predictors of happiness is something called *presence*. Presence means you are aware of what is happening as it is happening. If your child is lying on the couch watching TV and looking miserable, chances are good he or she *is* miserable—seeking distraction and not being present. Your child is not happy sitting there, vegging out in front of the TV.

A lot of kids grew up having been praised over and over again for the simplest things and never really tuned in to the experience.

"You drew me a picture! That's the most beautiful picture I have ever seen! You're a budding Picasso!"

If the parent changes the focus and says, "Look at the colors you chose. I really see how much energy you put into that and how excited you are to use so many different colors that go together! You really thought about that," the parent is identifying the experience the child brought to the effort as opposed to the final picture. Success is a process. Praise is great when it is about the process, not the product. Take twenty years of being praised for a product, add four years of getting good grades in college to the mix, and what do you have? The inevitable "Now what?" question—because you never tuned in to the process of someone identifying your effort and being appreciative or smiling because of that effort. If you happen to feel good about lying on the sofa because it beats bagging groceries, you have been overpraised for the product instead of the process.

Carol Dweck is one of the world's leading researchers in the field of motivation and is the Lewis and Eaton Professor of Psychology at Stanford University. Her research has focused on why people succeed and how to foster success. Her work says that there are two mind-sets—one is that you are born with talent and capacities and you either have them or you don't. The other says that you get your intelligence and talents by your effort. The population is divided between these two mind-sets roughly fifty-fifty. She has found that people who are raised with an innate mind-set that you are either "born with it" or not stop trying later in life, the thought being, "Why would I try, because if I try and I don't succeed, it is going to prove that I don't have it, so I am done." I call these people under-achievers.

People who are raised with the effort mind-set have a totally different approach: "They say that my brain is always changing based on my effort, so therefore, I am going to try." If this is the way your mind is set, you may not have found your perfect job yet, but there is an interest in developing something you have a passion for until you do.

Carol Dweck did a study in which she showed a half-hour video to a group of high school kids with the message that your effort determines your capacity to succeed. They showed the group a picture of how the brain changes when you face difficulties, make mistakes, and fail but explained this process as a good thing because it shows that you can work harder. After the class watched the video and heard the presentation, she divided the group in two. Some kids got the message and others didn't. The ones who got the message of the video had a zero dropout rate. They developed an understanding that trying and failing was much better than not trying at all.

I think this message is important for recent college graduates to know and understand. It's necessary to be aware of your inner life so you know what is exciting to you and where the fuel for your passion comes from. What are the areas you are going to put a lot of energy into? The world is too complex to do everything, so you've got to find your areas of passion.

There is a network of nerves around the intestines that gives you that "gut" sensation that can guide you. If you are not aware of these inner sensations of your body—called interception of the interior—you will find it nearly impossible to discover your true path in life. Asking you to find it would be the equivalent of asking a person who has no eyes to see. If you aren't aware of and in tune with what your body is telling you by developing this interior perception, you will have a very hard time answering the question "What's your passion?" You won't have any idea what that really means. Your answers will be something like these:

"I don't know who I am."

"I don't want to do anything."

"I am not going to go forward."

Assuming that you aren't clinically depressed or addicted to drugs, you can learn the process to develop inner awareness. Once you start doing that, you open yourself up to all sorts of possibilities that may become your passion. If you can develop the capacity to see the mind beneath the behavior, you can then be guided to create a healthy mind in yourself and in people around you.

Learning the Ropes

Throughout the process of writing this book, I have learned a huge number of great tips that will help me in life. I have kept track of the different tips as I have learned from my mistakes and experiences. I thought I would share them with you to pass on the knowledge with the hope that they will help you in the future—or, at the very least, maybe they will give you a good laugh.

- *Always respond to e-mails, even if you think the person sending the e-mail is unimportant. Just respond!*
- *Remember to always give an answer, even if the answer is "No." It's better to give some sort of an answer than nothing at all.*
- *Be prepared. If you are well prepared for something, you don't need to be nervous about messing up.*
- *Don't worry about not having it together, because not many people do. Many people who say they do actually don't.*

- *Don't ever think you know it all, because you don't and you never will.*
- *Be prepared for someone you thought would be amazing not to be and then learn from it.*
- *Realize that "rejection is God's protection."*
- *If you are ever talking to someone who goes off on a long ramble that you didn't plan for, don't stop it. Just shut up.*
- *Getting people to give you time is one of the biggest challenges in the world, so when you get a minute, be respectful of it and use it wisely.*
- *Don't think that because you find yourself interesting, everyone else will too.*
- *When you talk to someone who is rude to you for no reason, know that it has nothing to do with you and that they are really just pissed at themselves.*
- *Always make your own judgments of people—everyone has an opinion about someone, but let yourself be the real judge of another person.*
- *Know that after graduation, you will cry so many times trying to figure out who you are that people might label you as "emotionally fragile."*
- *Be prepared to go deep. You will find yourself asking questions like "Who am I?" and "What is my purpose on this earth?" and "What is my destiny?" It's all too crazy; have fun with it.*
- *At the end of the day, take a deep breath or scream into a pillow, because you will figure it out. I promise you!*

Now What?

If you've taken the time to read this book, then you're probably a lot like me. You're beginning a new chapter in your life. Maybe you feel daunted by all the possibilities before you and you're unsure of what you should do next. I am no stranger to these feelings. I wrote this book because of the anxiety I felt about finding a career. And writing this book turned out to be the perfect job for me at this moment in my life. It has given me the time I needed to help me understand and see my path more clearly. It made my first year out of college more understandable, and it has set me on a path that I feel positive about pursuing.

As a recent graduate, I feel a little silly offering life lessons. Instead, I'll tell you the four most important lessons I've learned from the people with whom I spoke.

1. It's okay not to know exactly what your life course will be.

I will admit that there are still times when I feel like

I have no idea what I am doing with my life. Sometimes I feel lost or that I am going off track, and I feel like I should be doing something else with my life. There were plenty of times during the process of writing this book when I asked myself, "Who am I to think I can write *this* book?" I had to keep reminding myself that if I was experiencing these feelings about life after college, other people my age were probably feeling similarly too.

By now, you've read that almost everyone in this book felt scared, confused, and unsure of what they were going to do after college, and most didn't have a specific plan when they graduated. When I graduated, I was beyond frustrated that I didn't have some sort of plan for myself. Today, I look back and am so thankful that I didn't have a set plan in place. If I had, I wouldn't have had the chance to write this book and learn so much from the people who gave me their time, advice, and wisdom along the way.

One of the greatest challenges I've had to face since I graduated from college is learning to be patient and having faith that I will find my place in the world. I often have to remind myself that I am still young and have a long life ahead of me. Now, at twenty-four, just starting out in my career, I realize I don't need to have it all figured out; I can enjoy being my age and continue to work hard and living in the moment, knowing that I have so much more to learn in life. I also know that my interests and ambitions will evolve as I get older and gain a deeper understanding of myself and of the world.

2. Be open to new possibilities.

I learned that it's best to be open-minded about opportunities that come your way; never close yourself off from things that may create happy accidents. If you do have a plan for your future, be prepared for it to change. Life is full of surprises, and it's best to be open to them. Be willing to adapt to whatever happens, because each apparent obstacle is a stepping-stone along the path that will lead you to where you are supposed to be. While I am still a planner and a list maker, I try to remind myself of the importance of also being open to the opportunities and things that aren't necessarily on my list. And if the winds of change should blow me in a new direction, I am confident that they will take me to wherever I am supposed to be. Stay curious, learn new things, and try things you never thought you would, because now is the time when your real education starts. Your textbook learning is done for now, but your life learning is just beginning. Think of this time as starting the University of Life.

3. It's okay to make mistakes.

I believe that everything happens for a reason. If you end up making mistakes along the way, see them as opportunities instead of setbacks. After all, you are in your twenties! It's not the end of the world. As most people in this book advised, make mistakes and give yourself permission to fail because this is the time to do that. You can re-create your life and the direction you are headed at any point in time.

4. Everyone's path is different.

It was reassuring to hear all the stories of the different paths that people traveled to get to where they are today. They may have gotten there through trial and error, but all of them discovered roles that gave their lives a sense of purpose and fulfillment. That can happen in the first five to ten years of your career, or it can happen later in life. Don't worry about there being a time limit—the discovery will come when you're ready.

After hearing all of these people's stories about not knowing how to deal with the "Now what?" question after graduation, you should feel comfort in knowing that you are not the only one feeling this way, and that you will survive. Some of us may have to dabble in a few more career paths than we expected, but that's okay too. It is all part of the journey.

———

I learned so much from interviewing everyone in this book, and I hope you did too. While I was excited and happy most of the time about this project and making the information I gathered accessible to those coming out of college, there were also times when I lost confidence. During the challenging moments—the moments when I was overcome by self-doubts and anxiety—I tried to keep my original goal in mind; I knew that if this book helped just one person overcome their anxieties and set out on their life's mission, then this book will have served its purpose.

I hope that you have been reassured that the fears

and doubts you may feel are a normal part of setting out into the world, and I wish you all the best on your journey today, and the journey of the next of the many "Now what?" questions that you will have throughout the rest of your life.

Acknowledgments

I would like to thank every person who gave me their time and the opportunity to interview them for this book; your stories and experiences have made this project what it is and will help countless people trying to find their way in life.

Thank you to my family and friends for dealing with me during this process and for being patient as I lived through my transition out of college and into the real world. I couldn't have done it without your undying love and support and your ability to make me laugh after many long days of work. Christina, thank you for adding humor to my life at all times and always finding some way to make me die of laughter. I love you and can't wait to see where life takes you. Patrick and Christopher, thank you for being the best roommates I could've asked for and dealing with my two a.m. lectures. I love you tons and can't wait to watch both of you graduate college and be asked, "So now what?" ☺

To my parents, who supported this idea from the beginning: thank you for sharing your experiences with me and for letting me interview you both for this book. A special thank-you to my mom for loving me through all of my moments of self-discovery and transformation; you are the greatest mother and best friend I could have ever dreamed of.

Thank you to my amazing book family: Jan Miller and Nena Madonia. This is our second book together and you are the greatest agents and friends a girl could wish for. To Laura Morton, a great writing partner and friend, who believed in me and this book; you kept me sane and always provided sarcasm and humor when it was needed. I couldn't have done this book without you. To my entire work family: Matthew DiGirolamo, Jon Liebman and Andrea Pett, Nadine Schiff, Justin Ongert, Jon Rosen, Mark Mullett, Stephanie Todoro, Jenn Beening, Rachel Jacobs, and Ashley Bekton. To Mary Choteborsky, my wonderful editor, who was patient and understanding the whole way through. And to everyone at Random House, thank you for taking a chance on me and this book. You gave me my first job out of college and have provided me with an experience that I will never forget during a time of immense growth and learning. I am forever grateful.